The Princess of Cleves. By Madame de La Fayette. Tr. by Thomas Sergeant Perry. With illustrations drawn by Jules Garnier, and engraved by A. Lamotte

de 1634-1693 La Fayette, Jean Regnauld de Segrais, François La Rochefoucauld, Thomas Sergeant Perry

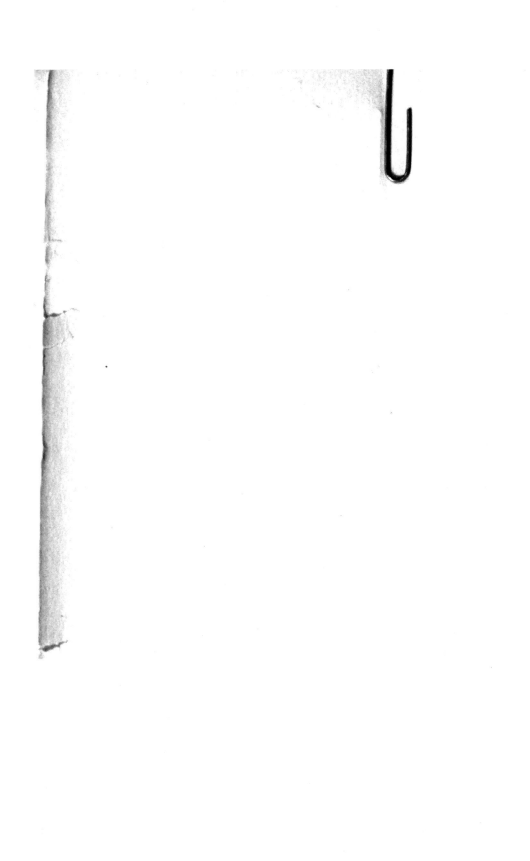

THE

PRINCESS OF CLÈVES.

THE

Princess of Clèves.

BY

MADAME DE LA FAYETTE.

TRANSLATED BY

THOMAS SERGEANT PERRY.

*WITH ILLUSTRATIONS DRAWN BY JULES GARNIER, AND
ENGRAVED BY A. LAMOTTE.*

IN TWO VOLUMES.

Vol. II.

BOSTON:
LITTLE, BROWN, AND COMPANY.
1891.

University Press:

John Wilson and Son, Cambridge.

CONTENTS TO VOL. II.

———•———

PART III.

WHEN peace was signed, Madame Elisabeth, though with great repugnance,
determined to obey her father the king. The
Duke of Alva had been deputed to marry
her in the name of the Catholic king, and
he was expected to arrive shortly. The
Duke of Savoy was also expected; he was
to marry Madame the king's sister, and the

two weddings were to take place at the same time. The king thought of nothing but making these events illustrious by entertainments at which he could display all the brilliancy and splendor of his court. It was suggested that plays and ballets should be sumptuously set upon the stage; but the king thought that too meagre a form of entertainment, and desired something more magnificent. He determined to have a tournament at which the foreigners might enter, and to admit the populace as spectators. All the princes and young noblemen gladly furthered the king's plan, and especially the Duke of Ferrara, Monsieur de Guise, and Monsieur de Nemours, who surpassed all others in exercises of this sort. The king chose them to be, with himself, the four champions of the tournament.

It was announced throughout the whole kingdom that a tournament would be opened in the city of Paris on the fifteenth day of June by His Very Christian Majesty

and by the Prince Alphonso of Este Duke
of Ferrara, Francis of Lorraine Duke of
Guise, and James of Savoy Duke of Nemours, who were ready to meet all comers.
The first combat was to be on horseback,
with four antagonists, with four assaults
with the lance, and one for the ladies; the
second combat with swords, either singly or
in couples, as should be determined; the
third combat on foot, three assaults with the
pike, and six with the sword. The champions were to supply the lances, swords, and
pikes, from which the assailants might choose
their weapons. Any one striking a horse in
the attack was to be put out of the ranks.
There would be four masters of the camp
who should have command, and those of
the assailants who should be most successful
would receive a prize, of a value to be determined by the judges. All the assailants,
French or foreign, were to be obliged to
come and touch one or more of the shields
hanging by the steps at the end of the lists;

there they would find an officer to receive and enroll them according to their rank and the shields they had touched. The assailants were to have a gentleman bring their shields with their arms, to be hung by the steps three days before the beginning of the tournament, otherwise they would not be received without the permission of the champions.

A great field was made ready near the Bastile, extending from the castle of Tournelles, across the Rue St. Antoine, to the royal mews. On each side scaffolding was raised, with rows of seats and covered boxes and galleries, fine to look upon, and capable of holding a vast number of spectators. All the princes and lords were thinking of nothing but their preparations to make a magnificent appearance, and were busily occupied in working some device into their initials or mottoes that should flatter the woman they loved.

A few days before the Duke of Alva's arrival the king went to play tennis with Monsieur de Nemours, the Chevalier de Guise, and the Vidame of Chartres. The queens went with their suites, and Madame de Clèves among the others, to watch the game. After it was over, and they were leaving the court, Châtelart went up to the dauphiness and told her that he had just found a love-letter that had fallen from Monsieur de Nemours' pocket. The crown princess, who was always curious about everything that concerned that prince, told Châtelart to give it to her; she took it, and followed the queen her mother-in-law, who was going with the king to see the preparations for the tournament. After they had been there some time the king sent for some horses which he had recently bought. Though they had not been broken, he wanted to mount them, and he also had them saddled for the gentlemen with him. The king and Monsieur de Nemours got on the most fiery ones, and they tried to spring at one another.

Monsieur de Nemours, fearful of injuring the king, backed his horse suddenly against a post with such violence that he was dismounted. The attendants ran up to him and thought he was seriously injured; Madame de Clèves thought him more hurt than did the others. Her interest in him inspired an agitation which she did not think of concealing; she went up to him with the queens, and her color was so changed that a man less interested than the Chevalier de Guise would have noticed it. He remarked it at once, and gave much more attention to the condition of Madame de Clèves than to that of Monsieur de Nemours. This prince was so stunned by the fall that his head had to be supported by those about him. When he came to himself, the first person he saw was Madame de Clèves; he read on her face all the pity she felt, and his expression showed that he was grateful. He then thanked the queens for their kindness, and apologized for appearing before them in such a state.

The king ordered him to go home and lie down.

After Madame de Clèves had recovered from her fright she began to recall the way she had betrayed it. The Chevalier de Guise did not leave her long to enjoy the hope that no one had observed it. As he gave her his hand to lead her from the field, he said: "I am more to be pitied, Madame, than Monsieur de Nemours. Pardon me if I abandon the profound reserve which I have always shown in regard to you, and if I betray the keen grief I feel at what I have just seen; it is the first time that I have been bold enough to speak to you, and it will be the last. Death, or at any rate an eternal separation, will remove me from a place where I cannot live, now that I have lost the sad consolation of believing that all those who dare to look upon you are as unhappy as I."

Madame de Clèves answered with a few disjointed words, as if she did not understand what the Chevalier de Guise meant. At any other time she would have been offended at his speaking of his feelings for her; but at that moment she thought only of her pain at perceiving that he had detected her own for Monsieur de Nemours. The Chevalier de Guise was so overwhelmed and pained by this discovery that he at once resolved never to think of winning Madame de Clèves' love; but the abandonment of a design which had seemed so difficult and glorious required one of equal moment to take its place, hence he thought of going to take Rhodes, — a plan he had already meditated. When he died, in the flower of his youth, just when he had acquired a reputation as one of the greatest princes of his century, his only regret was that he had not been able to carry out that noble project, which seemed on the point of accomplishment.

Madame de Clèves at once went to the queen, with her mind intent on what had just happened. Monsieur de Nemours came there soon afterward, in magnificent attire, as if he had forgotten what had just happened. He appeared even gayer than usual, and his delight at what he thought he had seen added to his content. Every one was surprised to see him, and asked him how he felt, except Madame de Clèves, who remained by the fire-place, as if she did not see him. The king came out of his room, and observing him there, called him to ask about his mishap. As Monsieur de Nemours passed by Madame de Clèves, he said in a low voice: "I have received to-day, Madame, tokens of your pity, but not those I most deserve." Madame de Clèves had suspected that the prince had noticed her emotion at his accident, and his words showed her that she was not mistaken. She was deeply pained to see that she could not control her emotions, and had even made them manifest to the Chevalier de Guise. It distressed her, too, to perceive that Monsieur de Nemours had read them; but this distress was tempered by a certain pleasure.

The dauphiness, who was impatient to know what was in the letter that Châtelart had given her, went up to Madame de Clèves. " Read this letter," she said; " it is addressed to Monsieur de Nemours, and apparently is from that mistress for whom he has left all the others. If you cannot read it now, keep it; come to me this evening and give it back to me, and tell me whether you know the handwriting." With these words the crown princess turned away from Madame de Clèves, leaving her so astonished and agitated that she could scarcely move. Her emotion and impatience were so great that she could not stay longer with the queen, and she went home, though it was much earlier than her usual hour of leaving. Her hands, in which she held the letter, trembled; her thoughts were all confused, and she felt an unendurable pain such as she had never known. As soon as she was

safe in her room she opened the letter, and
read as follows: —

"I love you too much to let you think
that the change you see in me is the result
of my fickleness; I want you to know that
the real cause is your infidelity. You are
surprised that I say your 'infidelity;' you
have concealed it so craftily, and I have
taken such pains to hide from you my
knowledge of it, that you are naturally astonished that I should have detected it. I
am myself surprised that I have been able
to keep it from you. Never was there any
grief like mine; I imagined that you felt
for me a violent passion. I did not conceal
what I felt for you, and at the time when
I let you see it, I learned that you were deceiving me, that you loved another, and,
according to all appearances, were sacrificing
me to a new mistress. I knew it the day
of the running at the ring, and that is why
I was not there. I pretended to be ill, in

order to conceal my emotion; but I really became so, for my body could not stand the intense agitation. When I began to get better, I pretended to be still suffering, in order to have an excuse for not seeing or writing to you; I wanted time to decide how I should act toward you. Twenty times at least I formed and changed my decision; but at last I judged you unworthy to see my grief, and I determined to hide it from you. I wished to wound your pride by letting you see my love for you fade away. I thought thus to diminish the price of the sacrifice you made of it; I did not wish you to have the pleasure of showing how much I loved you in order to appear more amiable. I resolved to write to you indifferent, dull letters, to suggest to the woman to whom you gave them that you were loved less. I did not wish her to have the pleasure of learning that I knew of her triumph over me, or to add to her triumph by my despair and reproaches. I thought I could not punish you sufficiently by breaking with you, and that I should inflict but a slight pain if I ceased to love you when you had ceased to love me. I thought you must love me, if you were to know the pang of not being loved, which tormented me so sorely. I thought that if anything could rekindle the feelings you had had for me, it was by showing that my own were changed, but to show this by pretending to hide it from you, as if I had not strength to tell you. I decided on this; but how hard it was to do so, and when I saw you, how almost impossible to carry it out! Hundreds of times I was ready to spoil all with my reproaches and tears. The state of my health helped me to conceal my emotion and distress. Afterward I was borne up by the pleasure of dissimulating to you as you dissimulated to me; nevertheless I did myself such violence to tell you and to write to you that I loved you, that you saw sooner than I had intended that I had not meant to let you see that my feelings were altered. You were wounded, and complained to me. I tried to reassure you, but in such an artificial way that you were more convinced than ever that I did not love you. At last I succeeded in what I had meant to do. The capriciousness of your heart made you turn again toward me when you saw me leaving you. I have tasted all the joy of vengeance; it has seemed to me that you loved me better than ever, and I have shown you that I did not love you. I have had reason to believe that you had entirely abandoned her for whom you had left me. I have also had grounds for supposing that you never spoke to her of me. But your return and your desertion have not been able to make good your fickleness; your heart has been divided between me and another; you have deceived me: that is enough to deprive me of the pleasure of being loved by you as I thought I deserved, and to fix me in the resolution that I had formed never to see you again, which so surprises you."

Madame de Clèves read and re-read this letter several times without understanding it; all that she made out was that Monsieur de Nemours did not love her as she had thought, and that he loved other women, whom he deceived as he did her. This was a grievous blow to a woman of her character, who was deeply in love, and had just shown this to a man whom she deemed unworthy, in sight of another whom she maltreated for love of his rival. Never was sorrow more bitter! It seemed to her that what had happened that day gave it a special sting, and that if Monsieur de Nemours had not had reason to suppose that she loved him, she would not care whether he had loved another woman. But she deceived herself; the pang she found so unendurable was that of jealousy, with all its hideous accompaniments. This letter showed her that Monsieur de Nemours had had a love-affair for some time. She thought that it attested the writer's cleverness and worth, and she

seemed a woman who deserved to be loved.
She appeared to have more courage than
herself, and she envied her the strength of
character she showed in concealing her feelings from Monsieur de Nemours. The end
of the letter showed that the woman thought
herself still loved; she imagined that his
constant discretion, which had so touched
her, was perhaps only the effect of his love
for the other, whom he feared to offend. In
a word, all her thoughts only fed her grief
and despair. How often she thought of
herself; how often of her mother's counsels! How bitterly she regretted that she
had not withdrawn from the world, in spite
of Monsieur de Clèves, or that she had not
followed her plan of confessing to him her
feeling for Monsieur de Nemours! She
judged that she would have done better to
tell everything to a husband whose generos-
ity she knew, and who would be interested
in keeping her secret, than to betray it to a
man unworthy of it, who was moved to love

of her by no other feeling than pride or vanity. In a word, she deemed every evil that could befall her, every misery to which she might be reduced, insignificant by the side of letting Monsieur de Nemours see that she loved him, and knowing that he loved another woman. Her only consolation was that henceforth she need have no fear of herself, and that she was entirely cured of her love for him.

She gave no thought to the dauphiness's command to come to her that evening; she went to bed and pretended to be indisposed, so that when Monsieur de Clèves came back from seeing the king, he was told that she was asleep. But she was far from enjoying the calmness that induces sleep. She spent the night in self-reproach and in reading over the letter.

Madame de Clèves was not the only person whose rest was disturbed by this letter. The Vidame of Chartres, who had lost it, not Monsieur de Nemours, was very uneasy

about it. He had spent the evening with
Monsieur de Guise, who had given a grand
supper to his brother-in-law, the Duke of
Ferrara, and all the young men of the court.
It so happened that during the supper the
conversation turned to bright letters, and
the Vidame said he had in his pocket the
brightest letter that ever was written. He
was asked to show it to them, but he refused.
Monsieur de Nemours thereupon declared
that he had never had it, and was only boast-
ing. The Vidame replied that he tempted
him to commit an indiscretion, but he would
not show the letter, though he would read a
few passages that would prove that few men
ever received one like it. At the same time
he felt for the letter, but could not find it; he
sought everywhere in vain. They laughed
at his discomfiture, but he seemed so uneasy
that they soon stopped talking about it. He
left before the others, hastening home to see
if he had left the missing letter there. While
he was still hunting for it, a first *valet de*

chambre of the queen came to tell him that
the Vicomtesse d'Uzès thought it well to
let him know that they were talking at the
queen's apartment about a love-letter he had
dropped from his pocket while he was play-
ing tennis; that they had repeated a good
deal that was in the letter; that the queen
had expressed a strong desire to see it; that
she had asked one of her gentlemen-in-wait-
ing for it; but he had answered that he had
given it to Châtelart.

The *valet de chambre* said many other
things to the Vidame which only added to
his distress. He went out at once to see a
gentleman who was a great friend of Châtelart; he made him get out of bed, although
it was very late, to go and ask for the letter,
without telling him who wanted it or who
had written it. Châtelart, who was con-
fident that it had been written to Monsieur
de Nemours, and that he was in love with
the dauphiness, felt sure that he knew who
had asked for it. He replied, with malicious

joy, that he had handed the letter to the dauphiness. The gentleman brought this answer back to the Vidame of Chartres; it gave him only fresh uneasiness. After long hesitation about what he should do, he decided that Monsieur de Nemours was the only man who could aid him.

The Vidame thereupon went to the house of the duke, and entered his bedroom at about daybreak. This prince was sleeping calmly; what he had seen that day of Madame de Clèves gave him only agreeable thoughts. He was much surprised when he was awakened by the Vidame, and he asked him whether this had been done out of revenge for what he had said at the supper. The Vidame's countenance showed that he had come on some serious matter. "I have come," he said, "to confide to you the most important event of my life. I know very well that you have no cause to be grateful, because I do this at a moment when I need your aid; but I know that I should have sunk in your esteem if without being compelled by necessity I had told you what I am about to say. Some time yesterday I dropped the letter of which I was speaking last evening; it is of extreme importance that no one should know that it was written to me. It has been seen by a number of persons who were at the tennis-court when I dropped it. Now, you were there too, and I beg of you to say that it was you who lost it."

"You must suppose that I am not in love with any woman," answered Monsieur de Nemours, smiling, "to make such a proposition to me, and to imagine that there is no one with whom I might fall out if I let it be thought that I receive letters of that sort."

"I beg you," said the Vidame, "to listen to me seriously. If you have a mistress, as I do not doubt, though I have no idea who she is, it will be easy for you to explain yourself, and I will tell you how to do it. Even if you do not have an explanation with her, your falling-out will last but a few moments ; whereas I by this mischance bring dishonor to a woman who has loved me passionately, and is one of the most estimable women in the world; and moreover, from another quarter I bring upon myself an implacable hatred, which will certainly cost me my fortune, and may cost me something more."

"I do not understand what you tell me," replied Monsieur de Nemours; "but you imply that the current rumors about the interest a great princess takes in you are not entirely without foundation."

"They are not," exclaimed the Vidame; "but would to God they were! In that case I should not be in my present trouble. But I must tell you what has happened, to give you an idea of what I have to fear.

"Ever since I have been at court, the queen has always treated me with much distinction and amiability, and I have reason to believe that she has had a kindly feeling for me; yet there was nothing marked about it, and I had never dreamed of other feelings toward me than those of respect. I was even much in love with Madame de Themines; the sight of her is enough to prove that a man can have a great deal of love for her when she loves him, — and she loved me. Nearly two years ago, when the court was at Fontainebleau, I happened to talk with the queen two or three times when very few people were there. It seemed to me that I pleased her, and that she was interested in all that I said. One day especially we were talking about confidence. I said I did not confide wholly in any one; that one always repented absolute unreserve sooner or later; and that I knew a number of things of which I had never spoken to any one. The queen said that she thought better of me for that; that she had not found any one in France who had any reserve; and that this had troubled her greatly, because it had prevented her confiding in any one; that one must have somebody to talk to, especially persons of her rank. The following days she several times resumed the same conversation, and told me many tolerably secret things that were happening. At last it seemed to me that she wanted to test my reserve, and that she wished to intrust me with some of her own secrets. This thought attached me to her; I was flattered by the distinction, and I paid her my court with more assiduity than usual. One evening, when the king and all the ladies had gone out to ride in the forest, she remained at home, because she did not feel well, and I stayed with her. She went down to the edge of the pond and let go of the equerry's hand, to walk more freely. After she had made a few turns, she came near me and bade me follow her. 'I want to speak to you,' she said, 'and you will see from what I wish to say that I am a friend of yours.' Then she stopped and gazed at me intently. 'You are in love,' she went on, 'and because you do

not confide in any one, you think that your
love is not known; but it is known even to
the persons interested. You are watched;
it is known where you see your mistress: a
plan has been made to surprise you. I do
not know who she is, I do not ask you; I
only wish to save you from the misfortunes
into which you may fall.' Observe, please,
the snare the queen set for me, and how
difficult it was to escape it. She wanted
to find out whether I was in love; and by
not asking with whom, and by showing that
her sole intention was to aid me, she prevented my thinking that she was speaking to
me from curiosity or with premeditation.

"Nevertheless, in the face of all appearances I made out the truth. I was in love
with Madame de Themines; but though she
loved me, I was not fortunate enough to
meet her in any private place where we could
be surprised, hence I saw that it was not she
whom the queen meant. I knew too that I
had a love-affair with a woman less beautiful

and less severe than Madame de Themines, and it was not impossible that the place where I used to meet her had been discovered; but since I took but little interest in her, it was easy for me to escape from perils of that sort by ceasing to see her. Hence I decided to confess nothing to the queen, but to assure her that I had long since given up the desire to win the love of such women as might smile on me, because I deemed them unworthy of an honorable man's devotion, and it would take women far above them to fascinate me. ' You are not frank,' replied the queen; ' I know the opposite of what you say. The way in which I speak to you binds you to conceal nothing from me. I want you to be one of my friends,' she went on; ' but when I give you that place, I must know all your ties. Consider whether you care to purchase it at the price of informing me; I give you two days to think it over. But be careful what you say to me at the expiration of that time, and remember that if I find out afterward that you have deceived me, I shall never pardon you so long as I live.' Thereupon the queen left me, without awaiting my reply.

"You may well imagine that I was much impressed by what she had just said. The two days she had given me for consideration did not seem to me too long. I perceived that she wished to know whether I was in love, and hoped that I was not. I saw the importance of the decision I was about to make. My vanity was not a little flattered by a love-affair with a queen, and a queen who was still so charming. To be sure, I love Madame de Themines, and although I was unfaithful to her in a way with that other woman I mentioned, I could not make up my mind to break with her. I also saw the danger to which I exposed myself in deceiving the queen, and how hard it would be to deceive her; yet I could not decide to refuse what fortune offered me, and I determined to risk the consequences of my evil conduct. I broke with that woman with whom my relations might be discovered, and I hoped to conceal those I had with Madame de Themines.

"At the expiration of the two days that the queen had granted me, as I was entering a room where all her ladies were assembled, she said to me aloud, with a seriousness that surprised me, —

"'Have you thought over that matter of which I spoke to you, and do you know the truth about it?'

"'Yes, Madame,' I replied, 'and it is as I told your Majesty.'

"'Come this evening at the hour that I shall write to you, and I will give you the rest of my orders.'

"I made a deep bow, without answering, and did not fail to appear at the hour set. I found her in the gallery with her secretary and some of her ladies. As soon as she saw me, she came up to me and led me to the other end of the gallery.

"'Well!' she said, 'is it after due reflection that you have nothing to say to me, and does not my treatment of you deserve that you should speak to me frankly?'

"'It is because I am frank with you, Madame,' I replied, 'that I have nothing to tell you; and I swear to your Majesty, with all the respect I owe you, that I am not in love with any lady of the court.'

"'I am willing to believe it,' resumed the queen, 'because I wish to; and I wish it because I desire that you should be unreservedly attached to me; and I could not possibly be satisfied with your friendship if you were in love. One may trust those who are, but it is impossible to have confidence in their secrecy. They are too inattentive and have too many distractions; their mistress is their main interest, — and that would not suit the way in which I want you to be attached to me. Remember, it is on account

of your oath that you are free that I choose
you for the recipient of my confidence.
Remember that I wish yours without reserve,
that I want you to have no friend, man or
woman, except such as shall be agreeable to
me, and that you will give up every aim except pleasing me. I shall not let harm come
to your fortune, — I shall look after that more
zealously than you do; and whatever I do
for you, I shall consider myself more than
paid if I find that you are to me what I hope.
I choose you in order to confide in you all
my anxieties, and to help me endure them.
You will see that they are not light. To all
appearance I suffer no pain from the king's
attachment to Madame de Valentinois; but
I can scarcely bear it. She controls the
king; she is false to him; she despises me;
all my people are devoted to her. My
daughter-in-law, the crown princess, is vain
of her beauty and of her uncle's power, and
pays no respect to me. The Constable of
Montmorency is master of the king and of

the kingdom; he hates me, and has given me tokens of his hatred which I can never forget. The Marshal of Saint-André is an audacious young favorite, who treats me no better than do the others. The full list of my sufferings would arouse your compassion. Hitherto I have not dared to trust any one; I do put confidence in you: act in such a way that I shall not repent of it, and be my sole consolation.'

"The queen's eyes filled with tears as she said these last words, and I was on the point of throwing myself at her feet, so deeply was I moved by the kindness she showed me. Since that day she has had perfect confidence in me; she never takes a step without talking it over with me, and my alliance with her still lasts.

PART IV.

" STILL, though much taken up by my new intimacy with the queen, I was bound to Madame de Themines by a feeling which I could not overcome. It seemed to me that her love for me was waning; and although if I had been wise I should have taken advantage of this change I saw in her to try to forget her, as it was, my love for her redoubled, and I managed so ill that the queen in time learned something about this attachment. Persons of her nation are always inclined to jealousy, and possibly her feelings toward me were warmer than she herself supposed. But at last the report that I was in love gave her such distress and grief that I very often felt sure that I had wholly lost her favor. I reassured her by my attentions, submissiveness, and by many false oaths; but I could not have long deceived her if Madame de Themines' altered demeanor had not at last set me free in spite of myself. She made me see that she loved me no longer, and I was so sure of this that I felt compelled to cease persecuting her with my attentions. Some time after, she wrote me the letter that I have lost. That told me that she knew about my relations with the other woman I mentioned, and that this was the reason of the change. Since, then, there was no one to divide my attentions, the queen was tolerably satisfied with me; but inasmuch as my feeling for her was not of a sort to render me incapable of another attachment, and it is impossible for a man to control his heart by force of will, I fell in love with Madame de Martigues, in whom I had been much interested before, when she was a Villemontais and maid-of-honor to the dauphiness. I had reason for believing that she did not hate me, and that she was pleased with my discreet conduct, although she did not understand all its reasons. The queen has no suspicions about this affair, but there is another which torments her a great deal. Since Madame de Martigues is always with the crown princess, I go there oftener than usual. The queen has taken it into her head that it is with this princess that I am in love. The dauphiness's rank, which is equal to her own, and her advantages of youth and beauty, inspire a jealousy which amounts to madness, and she cannot conceal her hatred of her daughter-in-law. The Cardinal of Lorraine, who seems to me to have been for a long time an aspirant for the queen's good graces, and who sees me occupying a place that he would like to fill, under the pretence of bringing about a reconciliation between her and the crown princess is looking into the causes of their dissension. I do not doubt that he has found out the real cause of the queen's bitterness, and I fancy that he has done me many an evil turn, though without showing his hand. That is the state of affairs now. Judge then what will be the effect of the letter I lost when I was unfortunate enough to put it into my pocket to return it to Madame de Themines. If the queen sees this letter, she will know that I have deceived her, and that at almost the same time when I was false to her on account of Madame de Themines, I was false to Madame de Themines on account of another woman. Judge then what sort of an opinion she will have of me, and whether she will ever believe me again. If she does not see this letter, what shall I say to her? She knows that it has been in the dauphiness's hands; she will think that Châtelart recognized that princess's handwriting, and that the letter is from her; she will imagine that she is perhaps the woman whose jealousy is mentioned, — in a word, there is nothing which she may not think, and there is nothing I may not fear from her thoughts. Add to this that I am sincerely interested in Madame de Martigues, that the crown princess will certainly show her this letter, and that she will believe it was written very recently. So I shall be embroiled both with the woman I love best in the world and with the woman from whom I have most to fear. Consider now whether I am not justified in begging you to say that the letter is yours and in asking you as a favor to try to get it from the dauphiness."

"It is very plain," said Monsieur de Nemours, "that one could hardly be in more serious perplexity than you are; and you must confess that you got into it by your own fault. I have been accused of being a faithless lover and of carrying on several love-affairs at the same time; but I am nothing by the side of you, for I should never have dreamed of doing what you have done. Could you suppose it possible to keep on good terms with Madame de Themines when you formed your alliance with the queen; and did you hope to become intimate with the queen and yet succeed deceiving her? She is an Italian and a queen, and hence suspicious, jealous, and haughty. When your good luck rather than your good conduct got you out of one entanglement, you got into a new one, and imagined that here, amid the whole court, you could love Madame de Martigues without the queen's knowing anything about it. You could not have been too careful to rid her of the mortification of having taken the first steps. She has a violent passion for you. You are too discreet to say so, and I am too discreet to ask any questions; but she loves you, she distrusts you, and the facts justify her."

"Is it for you to overwhelm me with reproaches?" interrupted the Vidame. "Ought not your experience to make you indulgent to my faults? Still, I am willing to confess that I did wrong; but consider, I beg of you, how to get me out of my present complications. It seems to me that you must see the crown princess as soon as she is up, and ask her for the letter as if it were yours."

"I have already told you," replied Monsieur de Nemours, "that this is a somewhat extraordinary request, and one that, the circumstances being what they are, I do not find very easy to grant. Then, too, if the letter was seen to fall from your pocket, how can I convince them that it fell from mine?"

"I thought I had said that they told the dauphiness that it was from yours that it fell."

"What!" said Monsieur de Nemours with some asperity, for he saw at once that this mistake might complicate matters with Madame de Clèves. "So the dauphiness has been told that I dropped this letter?"

"Yes," answered the Vidame; "that is what they told her, — and the mistake arose in this way: there were several of the queen's gentlemen in one of the rooms by the tennis-court where our clothes were hanging, and when we sent for them the letter dropped; these gentlemen took it up and read it aloud. Some thought it was written to you; others, that it was written to me. Châtelart, who took it, and from whom I have just tried to get it, said he had given it to the crown princess as a letter of yours; those who mentioned it to the queen unfortunately said it was mine, — so you can easily do what I wish, and get me out of this terrible complication."

Monsieur de Nemours had always been very fond of the Vidame of Chartres, and

his relationship to Madame de Clèves rend-
ered him still dearer.   Nevertheless, he could
not make up his mind to run the risk of her
hearing of this letter as something in which
he was concerned.   He began to meditate
profoundly, and the Vidame, guessing the
nature of his thoughts, said: " I really believe
you are afraid of falling out with your mistress; and I should be inclined to think that
it is about the dauphiness that you are
anxious, were it not that your freedom from
any jealousy of Monsieur d'Anville forbids
the thought.   But however that may be, you
must not sacrifice your peace of mind to
mine, and I will make it possible for you to
prove to the woman you love that this letter
was written to me, and not to you.   Here is
a note from Madame d'Amboise; she is a
friend of Madame de Themines, and to her
she has confided all her feelings about me.
In this note she asks me for her friend's
letter, — the one I lost.   My name is on the
note, and its contents prove beyond the

possibility of doubt that the letter she asks
for is the one that has been picked up. I
intrust this note to you, and I am willing
that you should show it to your mistress in
order to clear yourself. I beg of you not to
lose a moment, but to go to the dauphiness
this morning."

Monsieur de Nemours gave his promise
to the Vidame of Chartres and took Madame
d'Amboise's note. But his intention was
not to see the crown princess; he thought
he had something more urgent to do. He
felt sure that she had already spoken about
this letter to Madame de Clèves, and he
could not endure that a woman he loved so
much should have any reason for thinking
that he was attached to any other.

He went to her house as soon as he
thought she might be awake, and sent up
word that he would not ask to have the
honor at such an extraordinary hour if it
were not on very important business. Madame de Clèves was not yet up; she was

much embittered and agitated by the gloomy
thoughts that had tormented her all night.
She was extremely surprised when she heard
that Monsieur de Nemours wanted to see
her. Grieved as she was, she did not hesi-
tate to send him word that she was ill, and
unable to see him.

He was not pained by this refusal; an act
of coolness at a time when she might be
jealous was no unfavorable omen. He went
to Monsieur de Clèves' apartments and told
him that he had just called on his wife;
that he was very sorry he could not see her,
because he wished to speak to her of a matter of importance in which the Vidame of
Chartres was interested. In a few words he
told Monsieur de Clèves how serious the
matter was, and Monsieur de Clèves took
him at once to his wife's room. Nothing
but the darkness enabled her to hide her
agitation and surprise at seeing Monsieur de
Nemours brought into her room by her husband. Monsieur de Clèves said that there

was some question about a letter, and the
Vidame's interests required her aid; he
added that Monsieur de Nemours would tell
her what was to be done, and that he should
go to the king, who had just sent for him.

Monsieur de Nemours was left alone with
Madame de Clèves, — which was exactly
what he wanted. "I have come, Madame,"
he began, "to ask you if the dauphiness
has not spoken to you about a letter
which Châtelart gave her."

"She said something about it to me,"
answered Madame de Clèves; "but I don't
understand how this letter concerns my
uncle, and I am able to assure you that his
name is not mentioned in it."

"True, Madame," Monsieur de Nemours
went on, "his name is not mentioned; nevertheless, it was written to him, and it is of
the utmost importance to him that you
should get it out of her hands."

"I fail to understand," said Madame de
Clèves, "how it concerns him that this letter

should not be seen, and why it should be asked for in his name."

"If you will kindly listen to me," said Monsieur de Nemours, "I will speedily explain the matter to you, and you will soon see that the Vidame is so implicated that I should not have said anything about it even to the Prince of Clèves if I had not needed his assistance in order to have the honor of seeing you."

"I think that all that you might take the trouble to say to me would be useless," replied Madame de Clèves, somewhat tartly; "and it is much better that you should go to the crown princess and tell her frankly your interest in this letter, since it has been said that it belongs to you."

The vexation that Monsieur de Nemours saw in Madame de Clèves gave him the keenest pleasure he had yet known, and fully consoled him for his impatience to explain himself. "I do not know, Madame," he began, "what may have been said to the dauphiness; but this letter does not concern me personally, and it was written to the Vidame."

"That I believe," replied Madame de Clèves; "but the dauphiness has been told the contrary, and it will not seem to her likely that the Vidame's letters should fall out of your pockets. That is why, unless you have some good reason for concealing the truth from her, I advise you to confess it to her."

"I have nothing to confess to her," he went on; "the letter is none of mine, and if there is any one I wish to convince of this, it is not the crown princess. But, Madame, since the Vidame's fate is at stake, permit me to tell you some things which you will find quite worth listening to."

The silence of Madame de Clèves showed that she was willing to listen, and Monsieur de Nemours repeated in as few words as possible what the Vidame had told him. Although this might well have surprised,

or at least interested, her, Madame de Clèves
listened with such marked indifference that
she seemed to doubt it or to find it unworthy
of her attention. She maintained this indifference until Monsieur de Nemours mentioned Madame d'Amboise's note to the
Vidame of Chartres, which was the proof
of all he had just been saying. Since
Madame de Clèves knew that she was a
friend of Madame de Themines, it seemed
to her possible that Monsieur de Nemours
had been speaking the truth, and she began
to think that possibly the letter in question
had not been written to him. This thought
suddenly dispelled her indifference. The
prince read her the note, which exonerated
him completely, and then handed it to her
for examination, telling her that perhaps she
knew the handwriting; she was compelled
to take it and to read the address, and indeed every word, in order to make sure
that the letter asked for was the one in her
possession. Monsieur de Nemours said

everything he could think of to convince
her; and since a pleasant truth is readily believed, he succeeded in proving to Madame
de Clèves that he had no part whatsoever in
the letter.

Then she began to reflect on the Vidame's
troubles and danger, to blame his evil conduct, and to desire means to aid him. She
was surprised at the queen's behavior; she
confessed to Monsieur de Nemours that the
letter was in her possession, — in a word, so
soon as she thought him innocent, she inter·
ested herself at once with the utmost cordiality in the very things that at first left her
perfectly indifferent. They agreed that it
was not necessary to return the letter to
the crown princess, lest she should show it
to Madame de Martigues, who knew Madame
de Themines' handwriting, and would at
once have guessed, from her interest in the
Vidame, that the letter had been written to
him. They also thought that it was better
not to confide to the dauphiness the part

concerning her mother-in-law, the queen. Madame de Clèves, under the pretext of her concern for her uncle's affairs, gladly promised to keep every secret that Monsieur de Nemours might intrust to her.

This prince would have talked with her about other things than the Vidame's affairs, and would have taken advantage of this opportunity to speak to her with greater freedom than he had ever done, were it not that word was brought to Madame de Clèves that the dauphiness had sent for her; Monsieur de Nemours consequently was obliged to withdraw. He went to see the Vidame, to tell him that after leaving him he had thought it better to see his niece, Madame de Clèves, than to go straight to the dauphiness. He brought forward many good arguments in support of what he had done and to make success seem probable.

Meanwhile Madame de Clèves dressed in all haste to go to the crown princess. She had scarcely entered the room when the dauphiness called her to her, and said in a low voice,—

"I have been waiting two hours for you, and never had more difficulty in concealing the truth than I have had this morning. The queen has heard about the letter I gave you yesterday, and thinks it was the Vidame of Chartres who dropped it; you know she takes a good deal of interest in him. She wanted to see the letter, and sent to ask Châtelart for it; he told her he had given it to me, and then they came to ask me for it, under the pretext that it was a very bright letter, which the queen was anxious to see. I did not dare say that you had it; I feared she would think that it had been placed in your hands because the Vidame is your uncle, and that there was some understanding between you and me. It has already occurred to me that she did not like his seeing me often; so I said the letter was in the pocket of the clothes I wore yesterday, and that those who had the key of the room in which they were locked had gone out. So give me the letter at once, that I may send it to her; and let me look at it before I send it, to see if I know the handwriting."

Madame de Clèves was even more embarrassed than she had expected. "I don't know, Madame," she answered, "what you will do; for Monsieur de Clèves, to whom I had given it, gave it back to Monsieur de Nemours, who came this morning to get him to ask you to return it to him. Monsieur de Clèves was imprudent enough to say that it was in his possession, and weak enough to yield to Monsieur de Nemours' entreaties and to give it to him."

"You have put me in the greatest possible embarrassment," said the dauphiness, "and you did very wrong to return the letter to Monsieur de Nemours; since I gave it you, you ought not to have returned it without my permission. What can I say to the queen, and what will she think? She will believe, and on good grounds, that this letter concerns me, and that there is something between the Vidame and me. She will never believe that the letter belongs to Monsieur de Nemours."

"I am extremely sorry," answered Madame de Clèves, "for the trouble I have caused, — I see just how great it is; but it is Monsieur de Clèves' fault, not mine."

"It is yours," retorted the dauphiness, "because you gave him the letter. There is not another woman in the world who would confide to her husband everything she knows."

"I acknowledge that I was wrong, Madame," said Madame de Clèves; "but think rather of repairing than of discussing my fault."

"Don't you remember pretty well what was in the letter?" asked the crown princess.

"Yes, Madame," was the reply; "I remember it, for I read it over more than once."

"In that case, you must go at once and write it in a disguised hand. This copy I will send to the queen. She will not show it to any one who has seen the original; and even if she should, I shall always maintain that it was the one that Châtelart gave me, and he will not dare to deny it."

Madame de Clèves agreed to this plan, and all the more readily because she thought she would send for Monsieur de Nemours to let her have the letter again, in order to copy it word for word, and so far as possible imitate the handwriting; in this way she thought the queen could not fail to be deceived. As soon as she got home she told her husband about the dauphiness's embarrassment, and begged him to send for Monsieur de Nemours; this was done, and he came at once. Madame de Clèves repeated to him what she had just told her husband, and asked him for the letter. Monsieur de Nemours replied that he had already given it back to the Vidame de Chartres, who was so glad to see it again and to be out of danger that he had at once sent it to Madame de Themines. Madame de Clèves was in new trouble; but at last, after discussing the matter together, they determined to write the letter from memory. They locked themselves up to work, left word at the door that no one was to be let in, and sent off Monsieur de Nemours' servants. This appearance of mystery and of confidence was far from unpleasant to this prince, and even to Madame de Clèves. The presence of her husband and the thought that she was furthering the Vidame's interests almost calmed her scruples. She felt only the pleasure of seeing Monsieur de Nemours; it was a fuller and purer joy than any she had ever felt, and it inspired her with a liveliness and ease that Monsieur de Nemours had never seen in her, and his love for her was only deepened. Since he had never before had such pleasant moments, his own spirits rose, and when Madame de Clèves wanted to recall the letter and to write, he, instead of aiding her seriously, did nothing but interrupt her with idle jests.

Madame de Clèves was quite as merry; so that they had been long shut up together, and twice word had come from the dauphiness urging Madame de Clèves to make haste, before half the letter was written.

Monsieur de Nemours was only too happy to prolong so pleasant a visit, and forgot his friend's interests. Madame de Clèves was amusing herself, and forgot those of her uncle. At last, at four o'clock, the letter was hardly finished, and the handwriting was so unlike that of the original that it was impossible that the queen should not at once detect the truth; and she was not deceived by it. Although they did their best to convince her that the letter was written to Monsieur de Nemours, she remained convinced, not only that it was addressed to the Vidame de Chartres, but that the dauphiness had something to do with it, and that there was some understanding between him and her. This thought so intensified her hatred of this princess that she never forgave her, and persecuted her till she drove her from France.

As for the Vidame of Chartres, he was ruined so far as she was concerned; and whether it was that the Cardinal of Lorraine had already acquired an ascendency over her, or that the affair of this letter, in which she saw that she had been deceived, opened her eyes to the other deceptions of which the Vidame had been guilty, it is certain that he could never bring about a satisfactory reconciliation. Their intimacy was at an end, and she accomplished his ruin afterward at the time of the conspiracy of Amboise, in which he was implicated.

After the letter had been sent to the crown princess, Monsieur de Clèves and Monsieur de Nemours went away. Madame de Clèves was left alone; and as soon as she was deprived of the presence of the man she loved, she seemed to awaken from a dream. She thought with surprise of the difference between her state of mind the previous evening and that she then felt; she pictured the coldness and harshness she had shown to Monsieur de Nemours so long as she had supposed that Madame de Themines' letter had been written to him, and the tranquillity and happiness that had succeeded them when he had proved to her that this letter in no way concerned him. When she recalled that the day before she had reproached herself, as if it were a crime, for having shown an interest that mere compassion had called forth, and that by her harshness she had betrayed a feeling of jealousy, — a certain proof of affection, — she scarcely recognized herself. When she thought further that Monsieur de Nemours saw that she was aware of his love; when he saw that, in spite of this, she treated him with perfect cordiality in her husband's presence, — indeed that she had treated him with more kindness than ever before, that she was the cause of her husband's sending for him, and that they had just passed an afternoon together privately, — she saw that there was an understanding between herself and Monsieur de Nemours; that she was deceiving a husband who deserved to be deceived less than any husband in the world; and she was ashamed to appear so unworthy of esteem even before the eyes of her lover. But what pained her more than all the rest was the memory of the state in which she had passed the night, and the acute grief she had suffered from the thought that Monsieur de Nemours loved another and that she had been deceived.

Up to that time she had not known the stings of mistrust and jealousy; her only thought had been to keep from loving Monsieur de Nemours, and she had not yet begun to fear that he loved another. Although the suspicions that this letter had aroused were wholly removed, they opened her eyes to the danger of being deceived, and gave her impressions of mistrust and jealousy such as she had never felt before. She was astounded that she had never yet thought how improbable it was that a man like Monsieur de Nemours, who had always treated women with such fickleness, should be capable of a sincere and lasting attachment. She thought it almost impossible that she could ever be satisfied with his love. "But if I could be," she asked herself, "what could I do with it? Do I wish it? Could I return it? Do I wish to begin a love-affair? Do I wish to fail in my duty to Monsieur de Clèves? Do I wish to expose myself to the cruel repentance and mortal anguish that are inseparable from love? I am overwhelmed by an affection which carries me away in spite of myself; all my resolutions are vain; I thought yesterday what I think to-day, and I act to-day in direct contradiction to my resolutions of yesterday. I must tear myself away from the society of Monsieur de Nemours; I must go to the country, strange as the trip may seem; and if Monsieur de Clèves persists in opposing it, or in demanding my reasons, perhaps I shall do him and myself the wrong of telling them to him." She held firm to this resolution, and spent the evening at home, instead of going to find out from the dauphiness what had become of the Vidame's pretended letter.

When Monsieur de Clèves came home she told him she wanted to go into the country; that she was not feeling well, and needed a change of air. Monsieur de Clèves, who felt sure from her appearance that there was nothing serious ailed her, at first laughed at the proposed trip, and told her that she forgot the approaching marriages of the princesses and the tournament, and that she would not have time enough to make her preparations for appearing in due splendor alongside the other ladies. Her husband's arguments did not move her; she begged him, when he went to Compiègne with the king, to let her go to Coulommiers, — a country-house they were building at a day's journey from Paris. Monsieur de Clèves gave his consent; so she went off with the intention of not returning at once, and the king left for a short stay at Compiègne.

Monsieur de Nemours felt very bad at not seeing Madame de Clèves again after the pleasant afternoon he had spent with her, which had so fired his hopes. His impatience to meet her once more left him no peace; so that when the king returned to Paris he determined to make a visit to his sister, the Duchess of Mercœur, who lived in the country not far from Coulommiers. He proposed to the Vidame to go with him; the latter gladly consented, to the delight of Monsieur de Nemours, who hoped to make sure of seeing Madame de Clèves by calling in company with the Vidame.

Madame de Mercœur was delighted to see them, and at once began to devise plans for their amusement. While they were deer-hunting, Monsieur de Nemours lost his way in the forest; and when he asked what road he should take, he was told that he was near

Coulommiers.   When he heard this word, "Coulommiers," he at once, without thinking, without forming any plan, dashed off in that direction.   He got once more into the forest, and followed such paths as seemed to him to lead to the castle.   These paths led to a summer-house, which consisted of a large room with two closets, one opening on a flower-garden separated from the forest by a fence, and the other opening on one of the walks of the park.   He entered the summer-house, and was about to stop and admire it, when he saw Monsieur and Madame de Clèves coming along the path, followed by a number of servants.   Surprised at seeing Monsieur de Clèves, whom he had left with the king, his first impulse was to hide.   He entered the closet near the flower-garden, with the intention of escaping by a door opening into the forest; but when he saw Madame de Clèves and her husband sitting in the summer-house, while their servants stayed in the park, whence they could not reach him without coming by Monsieur and Madame de Clèves, he could not resist the temptation to watch her, or overcome his curiosity to listen to her conversation with her husband, of whom he was more jealous than of any of his rivals.

He heard Monsieur de Clèves say to his wife: "But why don't you wish to return to Paris? What can keep you in the country? For some time you have had a taste for solitude which surprises me and pains me, because it keeps us apart. I find you in even lower spirits than usual, and I am afraid something distresses you."

"I have nothing on my mind," she answered, with some embarrassment; "but the bustle of a court is so great, and our house is always so thronged, that it is impossible for mind and body not to be tired and to need rest."

"Rest," he answered, "is not needed by persons of your age. Neither at home nor at court do you get tired, and I should be rather inclined to fear that you are glad to get away from me."

"If you thought that, you would do me great injustice," she replied, with ever-growing embarrassment; "but I beg of you to leave me here. If you could stay too I should be very glad, provided you would stay alone, and did not care for the throng of people who almost never leave you."

"Ah, Madame," exclaimed Monsieur de Clèves, "your air and your words show me that you have reasons for wishing to be alone which I don't know, and which I beg of you to tell me."

For a long time the prince besought her to tell him the reason, but in vain; and after she had refused in a way that only redoubled his curiosity, she stood for a time silent, with eyes cast down; then, raising her eyes to his, she said suddenly, —

"Don't compel me to confess something which I have often meant to tell you, but had not the strength. Only remember that prudence does not require that a woman of my age, who is mistress of her actions, should remain exposed to the temptations of the court."

"What is it you suggest, Madame?" exclaimed Monsieur de Clèves. "I should not dare to say, for fear of offending you."

Madame de Clèves did not answer, and her silence confirming her husband's suspicions, he went on, —

"You are silent, and your silence tells me I am not mistaken"

"Well, sir," she answered, falling on her knees, "I am going to make you a confession such as no woman has ever made to her husband; the innocence of my actions and of my intentions gives me strength to do so. It is true that I have reasons for keeping aloof from the court, and I wish to avoid the perils that sometimes beset women of my age. I have never given the slightest sign of weakness, and I should never fear displaying any, if you would leave me free to withdraw from court, or if Madame de Chartres still lived to guide my actions. Whatever the dangers of the course I take, I pursue it with pleasure, in order to keep myself worthy of you. I beg your pardon a thousand times if my feelings offend you; at any rate I shall never offend you by my actions. Remember that to do what I am now doing requires more friendship and esteem for a husband than any one has ever had. Guide me, take pity on me, love me, if you can."

All the time she was speaking, Monsieur de Clèves sat with his head in his hands; he was really beside himself, and did not once think of lifting his wife up. But when she had finished, and he looked down and saw her, her face wet with tears, and yet so beautiful, he thought he should die of grief. He kissed her, and helped her to her feet.

"Do you, Madame, take pity on me," he said, "for I deserve it; and excuse me if in the first moments of a grief so poignant as

mine I do not respond as I should to your appeal. You seem to me worthier of esteem and admiration than any woman that ever lived; but I also regard myself as the unhappiest of men. The first moment that I saw you, I was filled with love of you; neither your indifference to me nor the fact that you are my wife has cooled it: it still lives. I have never been able to make you love me, and I see that you fear you love another. And who, Madame, is the happy man that inspires this fear? Since when has he charmed you? What has he done to please you? What was the road he took to your heart? I found some consolation for not having touched it in the thought that it was beyond any one's reach; but another has succeeded where I have failed. I have all the jealousy of a husband and of a lover; but it is impossible to suffer as a husband after what you have told me. Your noble conduct makes me feel perfectly secure, and even consoles me as a lover. Your confidence and your sincerity are infinitely dear to me; you think well enough of me not to suppose that I shall take any unfair advantage of this confession. You are right, Madame, — I shall not; and I shall not love you less. You make me happy by the greatest proof of fidelity that a woman ever gave her husband; but, Madame, go on and tell me who it is you are trying to avoid."

"I entreat you, do not ask me," she replied; "I have determined not to tell you, and I think that the more prudent course."

"Have no fear, Madame," said Monsieur de Clèves; "I know the world too well to suppose that respect for a husband ever prevents men falling in love with his wife. He ought to hate those who do so, but without complaining; so once more, Madame, I beg of you to tell me what I want to know."

"You would urge me in vain," she answered; "I have strength enough to keep back what I think I ought not to say. My avowal is not the result of weakness, and it requires more courage to confess this truth than to undertake to hide it."

Monsieur de Nemours lost not a single word of this conversation, and Madame de Clèves' last remark made him quite as jealous as it made her husband. He was himself so desperately in love with her that he supposed every one else was just as much so. It was true in fact that he had many rivals, but he imagined even more than there were; and he began to wonder whom Madame de Clèves could mean. He had often believed that she did not dislike him, and he had formed this opinion from things which now seemed so slight that he could not imagine he had kindled a love so intense that it called for this desperate remedy. He was almost beside himself with excitement, and could not forgive Monsieur de Clèves for not insisting on knowing the name his wife was hiding.

Monsieur de Clèves, however, was doing his best to find it out, and after he had entreated her in vain, she said: "It seems to me that you ought to be satisfied with my sincerity; do not ask me anything more, and do not give me reason to repent what I have just done. Content yourself with the assurance I give you that no one of my actions has betrayed my feelings, and that not a word has ever been said to me at which I could take offence."

"Ah, Madame," Monsieur de Clèves suddenly exclaimed, "I cannot believe you! I remember your embarrassment the day your portrait was lost. You gave it away, Madame, — you gave away that portrait which was so dear to me, and belonged to me so legitimately. You could not hide your feelings; it is known that you are in love: your virtue has so far preserved you from the rest."

"Is it possible," the princess burst forth, "that you could suspect any misrepresentation in a confession like mine, which there was no ground for my making? Believe

what I say: I purchase at a high price the
confidence that I ask of you. I beg of you,
believe that I did not give away the portrait;
it is true that I saw it taken, but I did not
wish to show that I saw it, lest I should be
exposed to hearing things which no one
had yet dared to say."

"How then did you see his love?" asked
Monsieur de Clèves. "What marks of love
were given to you?"

"Spare me the mortification," was her
answer, "of repeating all the details which
I am ashamed to have noticed, and have
only convinced me of my weakness."

"You are right, Madame," he said, "I am
unjust. Deny me when I shall ask such
things, but do not be angry if I ask them."

At this moment some of the servants who
were without, came to tell Monsieur de
Clèves that a gentleman had come with a
command from the king that he should be
in Paris that evening. Monsieur de Clèves
was obliged to leave at once, and he could

say to his wife nothing except that he begged
her to return the next day, and besought her
to believe that though he was sorely distressed, he felt for her an affection and
esteem which ought to satisfy her.

When he had gone, and Madame de Clèves
was alone and began to think of what she
had done, she was so amazed that she could
scarcely believe it true. She thought that
she had wholly alienated her husband's love
and esteem, and had thrown herself into an
abyss from which escape was impossible.
She asked herself why she had done this
perilous thing, and saw that she had stumbled
into it without intention. The strangeness
of such a confession, for which she knew no
precedent, showed her all her danger.

But when she began to think that this
remedy, violent as it was, was the only one
that could protect her against Monsieur de
Nemours, she felt that she could not regret
it, and that she had not gone too far. She
spent the whole night in uncertainty, anxiety,

and fear; but at last she grew calm. She felt a vague satisfaction in having given this proof of fidelity to a husband who so well deserved it, who had such affection and esteem for her, and who had just shown these by the way in which he had received her avowal.

Meanwhile Monsieur de Nemours had left the place where he had overheard a conversation which touched him keenly, and had hastened into the forest. What Madame de Clèves had said about the portrait gave him new life, by showing him that it was he whom she did not hate. He first gave himself up to this joy; but it was not of long duration, for he reflected that the same thing which showed him that he had touched the heart of Madame de Clèves, ought to convince him that he would never receive any token of it, and that it was impossible to gain any influence over a woman who resorted to so strange a remedy. He felt, nevertheless, great pleasure in having brought her to this extremity. He felt a certain pride in making himself loved by a woman so different from all others of her sex, — in a word, he felt a hundred times happier and unhappier. Night came upon him in the forest, and he had great difficulty in finding the way back to Madame de Mercœur's. He reached there at daybreak. He found it very hard to explain what had delayed him, but he made the best excuses he could, and returned to Paris that same day with the Vidame.

Monsieur de Nemours was so full of his passion and so surprised by what he had heard that he committed a very common imprudence, — that of speaking in general terms of his own feelings and of describing his own adventures under borrowed names. On his way back he turned the conversation to love : he spoke of the pleasure of being in love with a worthy woman ; he mentioned the singular effects of this passion ; and, finally, not being able to keep to himself his astonishment at what Madame de Clèves had done, he told the whole story to the Vidame, without naming her and without saying that he had any part in it. But he manifested such warmth and admiration that the Vidame at once suspected that the story concerned the prince himself. He urged him strongly to acknowledge this; he said that he had long known that he nourished a violent passion, and that it was wrong not to trust in a man who had confided to him the secret of his life. Monsieur de Nemours was too much in love to acknowledge his love; he had always hidden it from the Vidame, though he loved him better than any man at court. He answered that one of his friends had told him this adventure, and had made him promise not to speak of it, and he besought him to keep his secret. The Vidame promised not to speak of it; nevertheless, Monsieur de Nemours repented having told him.

Meanwhile, Monsieur de Clèves had gone

to the king, his heart sick with a mortal
wound. Never had a husband felt warmer
love or higher respect for his wife. What
he had heard had not lessened his respect,
but this had assumed a new form. His most
earnest desire was to know who had succeeded in pleasing her. Monsieur de
Nemours was the first to occur to him, as
the most fascinating man at court, and the
Chevalier de Guise and the Marshal of Saint-
André as two men who had tried to please
her and had paid her much attention; so
that he decided it must be one of these three.
He reached the Louvre, and the king took
him into his study to tell him that he had
chosen him to carry Madame to Spain; that
he had thought that the prince would dis-
charge this duty better than any one; and
that no one would do so much credit to
France as Madame de Clèves. Monsieur de
Clèves accepted this appointment with due
respect, and even looked upon it as something that would remove his wife from court

without attracting any attention; but the
date of their departure was still too remote
to relieve his present embarrassment. He
wrote at once to Madame de Clèves to tell
her what the king had said, and added that
he was very anxious that she should come
to Paris. She returned in obedience to his
request, and when they met, each found
the other in the deepest gloom.

Monsieur de Clèves addressed her in the
most honorable terms, and seemed well
worthy of the confidence she had placed
in him.

"I have no uneasiness about your conduct," he said; "you have more strength
and virtue than you think. It is not dread of
the future that distresses me; I am only distressed at seeing that you have for another
feelings that I have not been able to inspire
in you."

"I do not know how to answer you," she
said; "I am ready to die with shame when
I speak to you. Spare me, I beg of you,

these painful conversations. Regulate my conduct; let me see no one, — that is all I ask; but permit me never to speak of a thing which makes me seem so little worthy of you, and which I regard as so unworthy of me."

"You are right, Madame," he answered; "I abuse your gentleness and your confidence. But do you too take some pity on the state into which you have cast me, and remember that whatever you have told me, you conceal from me a name which excites an unendurable curiosity. Still, I do not ask you to gratify it; but I must say that I believe the man I must envy to be the Marshal of Saint-André, the Duke of Nemours, or the Chevalier de Guise."

"I shall not answer," she said, blushing, "and I shall give you no occasion for lessening or strengthening your suspicions; but if you try to find out by watching me, you will surely make me so embarrassed that every one will notice it. In Heaven's name,"

she went on, "invent some illness, that I
may see no one!"

"No, Madame," he replied, "it would
soon be found that it was not real; and moreover I want to place my confidence in you
alone, — that is the course my heart recom-
mends, and my reason too. In your present
mood, by leaving you free, I protect you by
a closer guard than I could persuade myself
to set about you."

Monsieur de Clèves was right; the confidence he showed in his wife proved a
stronger protection against Monsieur de
Nemours and inspired her to make austerer
resolutions than any form of constraint could
have done. She went to the Louvre and
visited the dauphiness as usual; but she
avoided Monsieur de Nemours with so much
care that she took away nearly all his happiness at thinking that she loved him. He
saw nothing in her actions which did not
prove the contrary. He was almost ready
to believe that what he had heard was a

dream, so unlikely did it appear. The only thing that assured him that he was not mistaken was the extreme sadness of Madame de Clèves, in spite of all her efforts to conceal it. Possibly kind words and glances would not have so fanned Monsieur de Nemours' love as did this austere conduct.

One evening, when Monsieur and Madame de Clèves were with the queen, some one said that it was reported that the king was going to name another nobleman of the court to accompany Madame to Spain. Monsieur de Clèves fixed his eyes on his wife when the speaker added that it would be either the Chevalier de Guise or the Marshal of Saint-André. He noticed that she showed no agitation at either of these names, or at the mention of their joining the party. This led him to think that it was neither of these that she dreaded to see; and wishing to determine the matter, he went to the room where the king was. After a short absence he returned to his wife and whis-

pered to her that he had just learned that it
would be Monsieur de Nemours who would
go with them to Spain.

The name of Monsieur de Nemours and
the thought of seeing him every day during
a long journey, in her husband's presence,
so agitated Madame de Clèves that she
could not conceal it, and wishing to assign
other reasons, she answered, —

"The choice of that gentleman will be
very disagreeable for you; he will divide all
the honors, and I think you ought to try to
have some one else appointed."

"It is not love of glory, Madame," said
Monsieur de Clèves, "that makes you dread
that Monsieur de Nemours should come with
me. Your regret springs from another
cause. This regret tells me what another
woman would have told by her delight. But
do not be alarmed; what I have just told
you is not true: I made it up to make sure
of a thing which I had only too long inclined
to believe." With these words he went

away, not wishing by his presence to add to his wife's evident embarrassment.

At that moment Monsieur de Nemours entered, and at once noticed Madame de Clèves' condition. He went up to her, and said in a low voice that he respected her too much to ask what made her so thoughtful. His voice aroused her from her revery; and looking at him, without hearing what he said, full of her own thoughts and fearful that her husband would see him by her side, she said: "In Heaven's name, leave me alone!"

"Alas! Madame," he replied, "I leave you only too much alone. Of what can you complain? I do not dare to speak to you, or even to look at you; I never come near you without trembling. How have I brought such a remark on myself, and why do you make me seem to have something to do with the depression in which I find you?"

Madame de Clèves deeply regretted that she had given Monsieur de Nemours an opportunity to speak to her more frankly than he had ever done. She left him without giving him any answer, and went home in a state of agitation such as she had never known. Her husband soon noticed this; he perceived that she was afraid lest he should speak to her about what had just happened. He followed her into her room and said to her, —

"Do not try to avoid me, Madame; I shall say nothing that could displease you. I beg your pardon for surprising you as I did; I am sufficiently punished by what I learned. Monsieur de Nemours was the man whom I most feared. I see your danger: control yourself for your own sake, and, if possible, for mine. I do not ask this as your husband, but as a man, all of whose happiness you make, and who feels for you a tenderer and stronger love than he whom your heart prefers." Monsieur de Clèves nearly broke down at these last words, which he could hardly utter. His wife was much moved, and bursting into tears, she embraced him with a gentleness and a sorrow that almost brought him to the same condition. They remained for some time perfectly silent, and separated without having strength to utter a word.

The preparations for Madame Elisabeth's marriage were completed, and the Duke of Alva arrived for the ceremony. He was received with all the pomp and formality that the occasion required. The king sent the Prince of Condé, the Cardinals of Lorraine and Guise, the Dukes of Lorraine, Ferrara, Aumale, Bouillon, Guise, and Nemours to meet him. They were accompanied by many gentlemen and a great number of pages wearing their liveries. The king himself received the Duke of Alva at the first door of the Louvre with two hundred gentlemen in waiting, with the constable at their head. As the duke drew near the king, he wished to embrace his knees; but the king prevented him, and made him walk by his side to call on the queen and on Madame Elisabeth, to whom the Duke of Alva brought a magnificent present from his master. He then called on Madame Marguerite, the king's sister, to convey to her the compliments of Monsieur de Savoie, and to assure her that he would arrive in a few days. There were large receptions at the Louvre, to show the Duke of Alva and the Prince of Orange, who accompanied him, the beauties of the court.

Madame de Clèves did not dare to stay away, much as she desired it, through fear of displeasing her husband, who gave her special orders to go. What made him even more determined was the absence of Monsieur de Nemours. He had gone to meet Monsieur de Savoie, and after that prince's arrival he was obliged to be with him almost all the time, to help him in his preparations for the wedding ceremonies; hence Madame de Clèves did not meet him so often as usual, and she was able to enjoy a little peace.

The Vidame of Chartres had not forgotten

the talk he had had with Monsieur de
Nemours. He had made up his mind that
the adventure this prince had told him was
his own, and he watched him so closely that
perhaps he would have made out the truth,
had not the arrival of the Duke of Alva and
of Monsieur de Savoie so changed and busied
the court that he had no further opportunity.
His desire for more information, or, rather,
the natural tendency to tell all one knows
to the woman one loves, made him mention
to Madame de Martigues the extraordinary
conduct of the woman who had confessed to
her husband the love she felt for another
man. He assured her that it was Monsieur
de Nemours who had inspired this violent
passion, and he besought her to aid him in
observing this prince. Madame de Martigues
was greatly interested in what the Vidame
had told her, and her curiosity about the
dauphiness's relations with Monsieur de
Nemours made her more anxious than ever
to get to the bottom of the affair.

A few days before the one set for the wedding the crown princess gave a supper to her father-in-law the king and the Duchess of Valentinois. Madame de Clèves, who was delayed in dressing, started for the Louvre a little later than usual, and on her way met a gentleman coming from the dauphiness to fetch her. When she entered the room the crown princess called out to her from the bed on which she was lying that she had been waiting for her with the utmost impatience.

"I fancy, Madame," she replied, "that I have no cause to be grateful to you for this impatience; it is doubtless for some other reason that you were eager to see me."

"You are right," said the dauphiness; "but, nevertheless, you ought to be obliged to me, for I am going to tell you something that I am sure you will be very glad to hear"

Madame de Clèves knelt down by the side of the bed in such a way that, fortu-

nately for her, her face was in the dark.
"You know," said the crown princess, "how
anxious we have been to find out the cause
of the change in the Duke of Nemours; I
think I have found out, and it is something
that will surprise you. He is desperately in
love with one of the most beautiful women
of the court, and the lady returns his love."

These words, which Madame de Clèves
could not take to herself, because she thought
that no one knew of her love for this prince,
gave her a pang that may be easily imagined.

"I see nothing in that," she replied,
"which is surprising for a man of his age
and appearance."

"But that," resumed the dauphiness, "is
not the surprising part; what is amazing is
the fact that this woman who loves Monsieur
de Nemours has never given him any token
of it, and that her fear that she may not
always be able to control her passion has
caused her to confess it to her husband to
persuade him to take her away from court.

And it is Monsieur de Nemours himself who is the authority for what I say."

If Madame de Clèves had been grieved at first by thinking that the affair in no way concerned her, these last words of the dauphiness filled her with despair, since they made it sure that it did concern her only too deeply. She could make no reply, but remained with her head resting on the bed while the dauphiness went on talking, too much taken up with what she was saying to notice her embarrassment. When Madame de Clèves had recovered some of her self-control, she answered, —

"This does not sound like a very probable story, and I wonder who told it to you."

"It was Madame de Martigues, who heard it from the Vidame. You know he is her lover; he told it to her as a secret, and he heard it from the Duke of Nemours. It is true that the Duke of Nemours did not mention the lady's name and did not even acknowledge that it was he who was loved;

but the Vidame de Chartres has no doubt about that."

As the dauphiness pronounced these last words, some one drew near the bed. Madame de Clèves was turned away so that she could not see who it was; but she knew when the dauphiness exclaimed, with an air of surprise and amusement, " There he is himself, and I am going to ask how much truth there is in it."

Madame de Clèves knew that it must be the Duke of Nemours, and so it was. Without turning toward him, she leaned over to the crown princess and whispered to her to be careful not to say a word about this adventure, that he had told it to the Vidame in confidence, and that this would very possibly set them by the ears. The dauphiness answered laughingly that she was absurdly prudent, and turned toward Monsieur de Nemours. He was arrayed for the evening entertainment, and addressed her with all his usual grace.

"I believe, Madame," he began, "that I can think, without impertinence, that you were talking about me when I came in, that you wanted to ask me something, and that Madame de Clèves objected."

"You are right," replied the, dauphiness; "but I shall not be as obliging to her as I usually am. I want to know whether a story I have heard is true, and whether you are the man who is in love with and is loved by a lady of the court who carefully conceals her passion from you and has confessed it to her husband."

Madame de Clèves' agitation and embarrassment cannot be conceived, and she would have welcomed death as an escape from her sufferings; but Monsieur de Nemours was even more embarrassed, if that is possible. This statement from the lips of the dauphiness, who, he had reason to believe, did not hate him, in the presence of Madame de Clèves, whom he loved better than any woman at court, and who also loved him, so overwhelmed him that he could not control his face. The embarrassment into which his blunder had plunged Madame de Clèves, and the thought of the good reason he gave her to hate him, made it impossible for him to answer. The dauphiness, noticing his intense confusion, said to Madame de Clèves: " Look at him, look at him, and see whether this is not his own story ! "

Meanwhile Monsieur de Nemours, recovering from his first agitation, and recognizing the importance of escaping from this dangerous complication, suddenly recovered his presence of mind and regained his composure.

" I must acknowledge, Madame," he said, " that no one could be more surprised and distressed than I am by the Vidame de Chartres' treachery in repeating the adventure of one of my friends which I told to him in confidence. I might easily revenge myself," he went on, smiling in a way that almost dispelled the dauphiness's suspicions;

" since he has confided to me matters of considerable importance. But I fail to understand why you do me the honor of implicating me in this affair. The Vidame cannot say that it concerns me, because I told him the very opposite. It may do very well to represent me as a man in love; but it will hardly do to represent me as a man who is loved, — which, Madame, is what you do."

Monsieur de Nemours was very glad to say something to the dauphiness which had some connection with his appearance in former times, in order to divert her thoughts. She caught his meaning; but without referring to these last words of his, she continued to harp on his evident confusion.

" I was embarrassed, Madame," he replied, " out of zeal for my friend and from fear of the reproaches he would be justified in making to me for repeating a thing dearer to him than life. Nevertheless, he only told me half, and did not mention the name of the woman he loves. I simply know that he is more in love and more to be pitied than any man in the world."

"Do you find him so worthy of pity," asked the crown princess, "because he is loved?"

"Are you sure that he is?" he answered; "and do you think that a woman who felt a real love would confide it to her husband? This woman, I am sure, knows nothing about love, and has mistaken for it a faint feeling of gratitude for his devotion to her. My friend cannot nourish any hope; but, wretched as he is, he has at least the consolation of having made her fearful of loving him, and he would not change his fate for that of any man in the world."

"Your friend's love is easily satisfied," said the crown princess, "and I begin to think that you can't be talking about yourself; I am inclined to agree with Madame de Clèves, who maintains that there can be no truth in the whole story."

"I don't think there can be," said Madame

de Clèves, who had not yet said a word; "and if it were true, how could it become known? It is extremely unlikely that a woman capable of such an extraordinary thing would have the weakness to tell of it. Evidently a husband would not think of doing such a thing, unless he were a husband very unworthy of the confidence that was placed in him."

Monsieur de Nemours, who saw that Madame de Clèves' suspicions had fallen on her husband, was very glad to strengthen them; he knew that he was his strongest rival.

"Jealousy," he replied, "and the desire to find out more than he had been told, may induce a husband to commit a great many indiscretions."

Madame de Clèves was at the end of her strength; and being unable to carry on the conversation further, she was about to say that she did not feel well, when, fortunately for her, the Duchess of Valentinois came in to tell the dauphiness that the king would arrive very soon. The crown princess accordingly went into her room to dress; whereupon Monsieur de Nemours came up to Madame de Clèves as she was about to follow her, and said, —

"Madame, I would give my life to speak to you a moment; but of all the important things I should have to say to you, nothing seems to me more important than to beg you to believe that if I have said anything which might seem to refer to the dauphiness, I have done so for reasons which do not concern her."

Madame de Clèves pretended not to hear him, but moved away without looking at him and joined the suite of the king, who had just come in. There being a great crowd present, her foot caught in her dress, and she made a misstep; she took advantage of this excuse to leave a place where she had no strength to stay longer, and went away pretending that she could not stand.

Monsieur de Clèves went to the Louvre, and being surprised not to see his wife, he was told of the accident that had just happened to her. He left at once, to find out how she was; he found her in bed, and she told him that she was but slightly hurt. When he had been with her for some time he saw that she was exceedingly sad; this surprised him, and he asked her, "What is the matter? You seem to suffer in some other way than that you have told me."

"I could not be in greater distress than I am," she answered. "What use did you make of the extraordinary, I might say foolish, confidence I had in you? Was I not worthy of secrecy on your part? And even if I was unworthy of it, did not your own interest urge it? Was it necessary that your curiosity to know a name which I ought not to tell you, could force you to confide in any one else in order to discover it? Nothing but curiosity could have led you to commit such an imprudence. The consequences have been most disastrous; the story is known, and has just been told to me, without any notion that I was the person most concerned."

"What do you say, Madame?" he replied. "You accuse me of having repeated what passed between us, and you tell me the story is known! I shall not defend myself from the charge of repeating it; you can't believe it, and you must have taken to yourself something said about some other woman."

"Oh, sir," she said, "in the whole world there is not another case like mine; there is not another woman capable of doing what I have done! Chance could not make any one invent it; no one has ever imagined it, —the very thought never entered any one's mind but mine. The dauphiness has just told me the whole story; she heard it from the Vidame of Chartres, and he had it from Monsieur de Nemours."

"Monsieur de Nemours!" exclaimed Monsieur de Clèves, with a gesture expressive of

the wildest despair. "What, Monsieur de
Nemours knows that you love him and that
I know it!"

"You always want to fix on Monsieur
de Nemours rather than any one else," she
replied; "I told you that I should never say
anything about your suspicions. I cannot
say whether Monsieur de Nemours knows
my share in this affair, or the part you assign
to him; but he told it to the Vidame de
Chartres, saying that he had it from one
of his friends, who did not give the name
of the woman. This friend of Monsieur de
Nemours must be one of your friends, and
you must have told the story to him in an
effort to get some information."

"Is there a friend in the world," he exclaimed, "to whom any one would make
a confidence of that sort? And would any
one try to confirm his suspicions by telling another what one would wish to hide
from one's self? Consider rather to whom
you have spoken. It is more likely that

the secret got out from you than from me. You could not endure your misery alone, and you sought solace in making a confidant of some friend who has played you false."

"Do not torment me further," she burst forth, "and do not be so cruel as to charge me with a fault which you have committed. Could you suspect me of that? And because I was capable of speaking to you, am I capable of speaking of it to any one else?"

His wife's confession had so convinced Monsieur de Clèves of her frankness, and she so warmly denied having mentioned the incident to any one, that Monsieur de Clèves did not know what to think. For his own part, he was sure that he had repeated nothing; it was something nobody could have guessed: it was known, and it must have become known through one of them. But what caused the liveliest grief was the knowledge that this secret was in somebody's hands, and apparently would be soon divulged.

Madame de Clèves' thoughts were nearly the same; she held it equally impossible that her husband should have spoken and should not have spoken. What Monsieur de Nemours had said, that curiosity might make a husband indiscreet, seemed to apply so well to just the state of mind in which Monsieur de Clèves was, that she could not think it was a mere strange coincidence; and this probability compelled her to believe that Monsieur de Clèves had abused her confidence in him. They were both so busy with their thoughts that they for a long time did not speak, and when they broke the silence, it was but to repeat what they had already said very often, and they felt farther apart than they had ever been.

It is easy to picture the way they passed the night. Monsieur de Clèves' constancy had been nearly worn out by his effort to endure the unhappiness of seeing his wife, whom he adored, touched with love for another man. His courage was wellnigh exhausted; he even doubted whether this was an opportunity to make use of it, in a matter in which his pride and honor were so sorely wounded. He no longer knew what to think of his wife; he could not decide what course of action he should urge her to take, or how he should himself act; on all sides he saw nothing but precipices and steep abysses. At last, after long distress and uncertainty, reflecting that he should soon have to go to Spain, he made up his mind to do nothing that should confirm any one's suspicions or knowledge of his unhappy condition. He went to Madame de Clèves and told her that it was not worth while to discuss which of them had betrayed their secret, but that it was very important to prove that the story that had been told was a mere invention in no way referring to her; that it depended on her to convince Monsieur de Nemours and the rest of this; that she had only to treat him with the severity and coldness which she ought to have for a man who made love to her, and that in this way she would soon dispel the notion that she had any interest in him. Hence, he argued, there was no need of her distressing herself about what he might have thought, because if henceforth she should betray no weakness, his opinion would necessarily change; and above all, he urged upon her the necessity of going to the palace and into the world as much as usual.

When he had finished, Monsieur de Clèves left his wife without awaiting her answer. She thought what he had said very reasonable, and her indignation against Monsieur de Nemours made her think it would be very easy to carry it out; but she found it very hard to appear at all the wedding festivities with a calm face and an easy mind. Nevertheless, since she had been selected to carry the train of the dauphiness's dress, — a special honor to her alone of all the princesses, — she could

not decline it without exciting much attention
and wonder. Hence she resolved to make a
great effort to control herself; but the rest of
the day she devoted to preparations and to
indulging the feelings that harassed her. She
shut herself up alone in her room. What
most distressed her was to have grounds for
complaint against Monsieur de Nemours,
with no chance of excusing him. She felt
sure that he had told the story to the Vidame, — this he had acknowledged; and she
felt sure too, from the way in which he spoke
of it, that he knew that she was implicated.
What excuse could be found for so great a
piece of imprudence, and what had become
of the prince's discretion, that had once so
touched her? "He was discreet," she said
to herself, "so long as he thought himself
unhappy; but the mere thought of happiness,
vague as it was, put an end to his discretion.
He could not imagine that he was loved without wishing it to be known. He has said everything he could say. I have not confessed

that it was he whom I loved; he suspected it, and showed his suspicions. If he had been sure of it, he would have done the same thing. I did wrong to think that there ever was a man capable of concealing what flattered his vanity. Yet it is for this man, whom I thought so different from other men, that I find myself in the same plight as other women whom I so little resemble. I have lost the love and esteem of a husband who ought to make me happy; soon every one will look upon me as a woman possessed by a mad and violent passion. The man for whom I feel it is no longer ignorant of it, and it is to escape just these evils that I have imperilled all my peace of mind, and even my life." These sad reflections were followed by a torrent of tears; but whatever the grief by which she felt herself overwhelmed, she knew that she could have endured it if she had been satisfied with Monsieur de Nemours.

This prince's state of mind was no more

tranquil.   His imprudence in unbosoming
himself to the Vidame of Chartres, and the
cruel results of this imprudence, caused him
great pain.   He could not without intense
mortification recall Madame de Clèves' agitation and embarrassment.   He could not forgive himself for having spoken about that
affair in terms which, though courteous in
themselves, must have seemed coarse and
impolite, since they had implied to Madame
de Clèves that he knew that she was the
woman who was deeply in love, and with
him.   All that he could wish was a conversation with her; but he thought this more
to be dreaded than desired.   " What should
I have to say to her ? " he exclaimed.
" Should I once more undertake to tell her
what I have already made too clear to her ?
Shall I let her see that I know she loves
me, — I, who have never dared to tell her
that I loved her?   Shall I begin by speaking to her openly of my passion, in order to
appear like a man emboldened by hope?

Can I think merely of going near her, and should I dare to embarrass her by my presence? How could I justify myself? I have no excuse, I am unworthy to appear before Madame de Clèves, and I do not venture to hope that she will ever look at me again. By my own fault, I have given her a better protection against me than any she sought, and sought perhaps in vain. By my imprudence I have lost the happiness and pride of being loved by the most charming and estimable woman in the world. If I had lost this happiness without her suffering, without having inflicted on her a bitter blow, that would be some consolation; and at this moment I feel more keenly the harm I have done her than I did when I was in her presence."

Monsieur de Nemours long tortured himself with these thoughts. The desire to see Madame de Clèves perpetually haunted him, and he began to look about for means of communicating with her. He thought of writing to her; but he considered, after his blunder, and in view of her character, that the best thing he could do would be to show his profound respect, and by silence and evident distress to make it clear that he did not dare to meet her, and to wait until time, chance, or her own interest in him should work in his favor. He resolved also to forbear from reproaching the Vidame of Chartres for his treachery, lest he should confirm his suspicions.

The betrothal of Madame Elisabeth, which was to take place on the morrow, and the wedding, which was to be celebrated on the following day, so occupied the court that Madame de Clèves and Monsieur de Nemours had no difficulty in concealing their grief and annoyance from the public. The dauphiness referred only lightly to their talk with Monsieur de Nemours, and Monsieur de Clèves took pains not to say anything more to his wife about what had happened, so that soon she found herself more at ease than she had supposed possible.

The betrothal was celebrated at the Louvre; and after the banquet and the ball, the whole royal household went to the bishop's palace to pass the night, as was the custom. The next morning the Duke of Alva, who always dressed very simply, put on a coat of cloth of gold, mingled with red, yellow, and black, and all covered with precious stones; on his head he wore a crown. The Prince of Orange, arrayed in equal splendor, came with his servants, and all the Spaniards with theirs, to fetch the Duke of Alva from the Villeroy mansion, where he was staying; and they started, walking four abreast, for the bishop's palace. As soon as they arrived, they went in due order to the church. The king conducted Madame Elisabeth, who also wore a crown; her dress was held by Mesdemoiselles de Montpensier and De Longueville; then came the queen, but not wearing a crown; after her came the dauphiness, the king's sister, Madame de Lorraine, and the Queen of

Navarre, with princesses holding their trains. The queens and princesses had all their maids-of-honor magnificently dressed in the same colors that they themselves wore, so that the maids-of-honor could be at once distinguished by the colors of their dresses. They ascended the platform set up in the church, and the wedding ceremony took place. Then they returned to dinner at the bishop's palace, and at about five left for the palace, to be present at the banquet to which the parliament, the sovereign courts, and the city officials had been invited. The king, the queens, the princes, and princesses ate at the marble table in the great hall of the palace, the Duke of Alva being seated near the new Queen of Spain. Below the steps of the marble table, on the king's right hand, was a table for the ambassadors, the archbishops, and the knights of the order, and on the other side a table for the members of parliament.

The Duke of Guise, dressed in a robe

of cloth of gold, was the king's major-domo, the Prince of Condé his head butler, the Duke of Nemours his cupbearer. After the tables were removed, the ball began; it was interrupted by the ballets and by extraordinary shows; then it was renewed, until, after midnight, the king and all the court returned to the Louvre. Though Madame de Clèves was very much depressed, she yet appeared in the eyes of every one, and especially in those of Monsieur de Nemours, incomparably beautiful. He did not dare to speak to her, although the confusion of the ceremony gave him many opportunities; but his demeanor was so dejected, and he showed such fear of approaching her, that she began to deem him less blameworthy, though he had not said a word in excuse of his conduct. His behavior was the same on the succeeding days, and continued to produce the same impression on Madame de Clèves.

At last the day of the tournament came. The queens betook themselves to the galleries and the raised seats set apart for them. The four champions appeared at the end of the lists, with a number of horses and servants, who formed the most magnificent spectacle ever seen in France.

The king's colors were plain black and white, which he always wore for the sake of Madame de Valentinois, who was a widow. The Duke of Ferrara and all his suite wore yellow and red. Monsieur de Guise appeared in pink and white: no one knew why he wore these colors; but it was remembered that they were those of a beautiful woman whom he had loved before she was married, and still loved, though he did not dare to show it. Monsieur de Nemours wore yellow and black, — why, no one knew. Madame de Clèves, however, had no difficulty in guessing: she remembered telling him one day that she liked yellow, and was sorry she was a blonde, because she could never wear that color. He believed that he could appear in it without indiscretion, because since Madame de Clèves never wore it, no one could suspect that it was hers.

Never was there seen greater skill than the four champions displayed. Although the king was the best horseman in the kingdom, it was hard to know to whom to give the palm. Monsieur de Nemours showed a grace in all he did that inclined in his favor women less interested than Madame de Clèves. As soon as she saw him at the end of the lists she felt an unusual emotion, and every time he ran she could scarcely conceal her joy when he escaped without harm.

Toward evening, when all was nearly over, and the company on the point of withdrawing, the evil fate of the country made the king wish to break another lance. He ordered the Count of Montgomery, who was very skilful, to enter the lists. The count begged the king to excuse him, and made every apology he could think of; but the king, with some annoyance, sent him word that he insisted upon it. The queen sent a message to the king beseeching him not to run again, saying that he had done so well he ought to be satisfied, and that she entreated him to come to her. He answered that it was for love of her that he was going to run again, and entered the field. She sent Monsieur de Savoie to beg him again to come; but all was in vain. He started, the lances broke, and a splinter from that of the Count of Montgomery struck him in the eye and remained in it. He fell at once to the ground. His equerries and Monsieur de Montgomery, one of the marshals of the field, ran up to him, and were alarmed to see him so severely wounded. The king was not alarmed; he said it was a slight matter, and that he forgave the count. It is easy to conceive the excitement and distress caused by this unhappy accident after a day devoted to merry-making. As soon as the king had been carried to his bed the surgeons examined his wound, which they found very serious. The constable at that moment recalled the prediction made to the king that he should be slain in single combat, and he had no doubt that the prophecy would come true.

As soon as the King of Spain, who was then in Brussels, heard of this accident, he sent his physician, a man of vast experience; but he thought the king's state desperate.

The court, thus distracted and torn by conflicting interests, was much excited on the eve of this great event; but all dissensions were quieted, and there seemed to be no other cause of anxiety than the king's health. The queens, the princes, and the princesses scarcely left his ante-chamber.

Madame de Clèves, knowing that she was compelled to be there and to meet Monsieur de Nemours, and that she could not hide from her husband the embarrassment that the sight of him would produce; knowing too that the mere presence of this prince would excuse him and overthrow all her plans, — decided to feign illness. The court was too busy to notice her conduct or to make out how much was true and how much feigned in her illness. Her husband alone could know the truth; but she was not sorry to have him know it, so she remained at home, thinking little of the great change that was impending, and perfectly free to indulge in her own reflections. Every one was with the king. Monsieur de Clèves came at certain hours to tell her the news. He treated her as he had always done, except that when they were alone his manner was a little colder and stiffer. He never spoke to her again about what had happened, and she lacked the strength and deemed it unwise to reopen the subject.

Monsieur de Nemours, who had expected to find a few moments to speak to Madame de Clèves, was much surprised and pained not to have even the pleasure of seeing her. The king grew so much worse that on the seventh day his physicians gave him up. He received the news of his approaching death with wonderful firmness, all the more admirable because he died by such an unfortunate accident, in the prime of life, full of happiness, adored by his subjects, and loved by a mistress whom he madly worshipped. The evening before his death he had Madame his sister married with Monsieur de Savoie, very quietly.

It is easy to conceive in what state was Madame de Valentinois. The queen did not permit her to see the king, and sent to her to ask for the king's seals and for the crown jewels, which were in her keeping. The duchess asked if the king was dead; and when they told her no, she said: "Then I have no master, and no one can compel me to return what he intrusted to my hands."

As soon as he had died, at the castle of Tournelles, the Duke of Ferrara, the Duke of Guise, and the Duke of Nemours conducted to the Louvre the queen-dowager, the king,

and his wife the queen. Monsieur de Nemours escorted the queen-dowager. Just as
they were starting, she drew back a little and
told her daughter-in-law she was to go first;
but it was easy to see that there was more
vexation than politeness in this compliment.

PART V.

THE Cardinal of Lorraine had acquired complete ascendency over the mind of the queen-dowager; the Vidame de Chartres had completely fallen from her good graces, but his love for Madame de Martigues and his enjoyment of his freedom had prevented him from suffering from this change as much as he might have done. During the ten days of the king's illness the cardinal had had abundant leisure to

form his plans and to persuade the queen
to take measures in conformity with his pro-
jects; hence as soon as the king was dead, the
queen ordered the constable to remain at
the castle of Tournelles to keep watch by
the body of the late king and to take charge
of the customary ceremonies. This order
kept him aloof from everything, and prevented all action on his part. He sent a
messenger to the King of Navarre to summon
him in all diligence, in order that they might
combine to oppose the promotion that
evidently awaited the Guises. The command of the army was given to the Duke
of Guise; that of the treasury to the Cardinal of Lorraine; the Duchess of Valentinois
was driven from the court; the Cardinal of
Tournon, the avowed enemy of the constable, was recalled, as well as the Chancelier
Olivier, the open enemy of the Duchess of
Valentinois, so that the aspect of the court
was completely changed. The Duke of
Guise was made equal to the princes of the

blood, and allowed to carry the king's mantle at the funeral; he and his brothers were placed high in authority, not merely through the cardinal's influence over the queen, but also because she believed that she could overthrow them if they should offend her, while she would not be able to overthrow the constable, who was supported by the princes of the blood.

After the funeral the constable went to the Louvre, but met with a cold reception from the king. He desired to speak with the king in private; but the king called the Guises and told him in their presence that he advised him to seek retirement, that the treasury and the command of the army were already disposed of, and that whenever he might need his counsels he should summon him. The queen-dowager received him even more coldly than the king; she went so far as to remind him of his insulting remark to the late king about his children not looking like him. The King of Navarre

arrived, and was received no better. The
Prince of Condé, who was less patient than
his brother, complained bitterly, but all in
vain; he was exiled from court under the
pretext of sending him to Flanders to sign
the ratification of the treaty of peace.
The King of Navarre was shown a forged
letter of the King of Spain which accused
him of making attempts on his territory, and
he was made to fear for his own possessions,
and induced to return to his kingdom. The
queen made this easy for him by assigning
to him the duty of escorting Madame Elisabeth; she even obliged him to start before
her, so that there was no one left at court
to oppose the power of the household of
Guise.

Although it was most unfortunate for
Monsieur de Clèves that he could not escort Madame Elisabeth, he still could not
complain, in view of the lofty rank of the
man who was preferred; but the depriva-
tion of the dignity was not what pained

him, but rather that his wife lost an opportunity of absenting herself from court without exciting comment.

A few days after the king's death it was decided that the court should go to Rheims for the coronation. Madame de Clèves, who had hitherto stayed at home under pretence of illness, begged her husband to excuse her from accompanying the court, and to let her go to Coulommiers to get strength from the change of air. He replied that he would not ask her whether it was care for her health that compelled her to give up the journey, but that he was willing she should not take it. He readily consented to a plan he had already decided on. High as was his opinion of his wife's virtue, he saw very clearly that it was not well for her to be exposed longer to meeting a man she loved.

Monsieur de Nemours soon learned that Madame de Clèves was not to accompany the court. He could not bear to think of leaving without seeing her; and the day before he was to start he called on her as late as he could, in order to find her alone. Fortune favored him, and as he entered the courtyard he met Madame de Nevers and Madame de Martigues coming out. They told him they had left her alone. He went upstairs in a state of agitation that can only be compared with that of Madame de Clèves when his name was announced. Her fear that he would mention his love; her apprehension lest she should give him a favorable answer; the anxiety that this visit would give her husband; the difficulty of repeating or concealing everything that happened, — all crowded on her mind at once, and so embarrassed her that she determined to avoid the thing she desired most in the world. She sent one of her maids to Monsieur de Nemours, who was in the hall, to tell him that she was not feeling well, and much regretted that she could not have the honor

of receiving him. It was a grievous blow
to him that he could not see Madame de
Clèves because she was unwilling to receive
him. He was to leave the next day,
and there was no chance of his meeting
her. He had not spoken to her since their
conversation at the crown princess's, and
he had reason to believe that his mistake
in speaking to the Vidame had shattered
all his hopes; consequently, he went away
in deep dejection.

As soon as Madame de Clèves had somewhat recovered from the agitation of the
prince's threatened visit, all the arguments
that had made her decline it vanished from
her mind; she even thought she had made
a mistake, and if she had dared, and there
had still been time, she would have called
him back.

Madame de Nevers and Madame de Martigues, after leaving her, went to the crown
princess's and found Monsieur de Clèves
there. The princess asked them where

they had been. They said they had just
come from Madame de Clèves', where they
had spent the afternoon with a number of
persons, and that they had left no one there
except Monsieur de Nemours. These words,
which they thought thoroughly insignificant, were quite the opposite for Monsieur de Clèves, although it must have
been evident to him that Monsieur de
Nemours could easily find opportunities to
speak to his wife. Nevertheless, the thought
that he was with her alone, and able to
speak to her of his love, seemed to him at
that moment such a new and unendurable
thing that his jealousy flamed out with
greater fury than ever. He was not able
to stay longer with the dauphiness, but left,
not knowing why he did so, or whether he
meant to interrupt Monsieur de Nemours.
As soon as he got home he looked to see
if that gentleman was still there; and when
he had the consolation of finding him gone,
he rejoiced to think that he could not have

stayed long. He fancied that perhaps it was not Monsieur de Nemours of whom he ought to be jealous; and although he did not really doubt it, he tried his best to do so: but so many things pointed in that direction that he could not long enjoy the happiness of uncertainty. He went straight to his wife's room, and after a little talk on indifferent matters, he could not refrain from asking her what she had done and whom she had seen. Observing that she did not mention Monsieur de Nemours, he asked her, trembling with excitement, if those were all she had seen, in order to give her an opportunity to mention him, and thus save him from the pain of thinking she was capable of deception. Since she had not seen him, she said nothing about him; whereupon Monsieur de Clèves, in a tone that betrayed his distress, asked:

"And Monsieur de Nemours, did n't you see him, or have you forgotten him?"

"I did not see him, in point of fact; I

was not feeling well, and I sent my regrets by one of my maids."

"Then you were ill for him alone," he went on, "since you received everybody else? Why this difference for him? Why is he not the same to you as all the rest? Why should you dread meeting him? Why do you show him that you make use of the power his passion gives you over him? Would you dare to refuse to see him if you did not know that he is able to distinguish your severity from incivility? Why should you be severe to him? From a person in your position, Madame, everything is a favor except indifference."

"I never thought," answered Madame de Clèves, "that however suspicious you might be of Monsieur de Nemours, you would reproach me for not seeing him."

"I do, however," he went on, "and with good cause. Why do you decline to see him, if he has not said anything to you? But, Madame, he has spoken to you; had his silence been the only sign of his passion, it would have made no such deep impression. You have not been able to tell me the whole truth; you have even repented telling me the little you did, and you have not the strength to go on. I am more unhappy than I supposed, — I am the unhappiest of men. You are my wife, I love you devotedly, and I see you love another man! He is the most fascinating man at court, he sees you every day, he knows that you love him. And I," he exclaimed, — "I could bring myself to believe that you would overcome your passion for him! I must have lost my reason when I imagined such a thing possible."

"I don't know," replied Madame de Clèves, sadly, "whether you were wrong in judging such extraordinary conduct as mine so favorably; I don't feel sure that I was right in thinking that you would do me justice."

"Do not doubt it, Madame," said Monsieur de Clèves. "You were mistaken; you expected of me things quite as impossible as what I expected of you. How could you expect me to retain my self-control? Have you forgotten that I loved you madly and that I was your husband? Either case is enough to drive a man wild: what must it be when the two combine? And see what they do! I am torn by wild and uncertain feelings that I cannot control; I find myself no longer worthy of you, — you seem no more worthy of me. I adore you, and I hate you; I offend you, and I beg your pardon; I admire you, and I am ashamed of my admiration, — in a word, I have lost all my calmness, all my reason. I do not know how I have been able to live since you spoke with me at Coulommiers, and since the day when you learned from the dauphiness that your adventure was known. I cannot conjecture how it came out, or what passed between Monsieur de Nemours and you on this subject. You will never tell me, and I don't ask you to tell me; I beg of you only to remember that you have made me the unhappiest man in the world."

With those words Monsieur de Clèves left his wife's room, and went away the next morning without seeing her, although he wrote her a letter full of grief, consideration, and gentleness. She wrote him a touching answer, containing such assurances about her past and future conduct that, since they sprang from the truth and were her real feelings, the letter carried great weight with Monsieur de Clèves and calmed him somewhat. Moreover, since Monsieur de Nemours was also on his way to join the king, her husband had the consolation of knowing that he was separated from Madame de Clèves. Whenever she spoke with her husband, the love he showed her, the uprightness of his treatment of her, her own affection for him, and her sense of duty, made an impression on her heart which effaced all thought of

Monsieur de Nemours. But this was only
for a time; the remembrance of him soon
returned with greater force than ever.

The first days after that prince had left,
she scarcely noticed his absence; then it began to appear painful, — for since she began
to love him, hardly a day had passed in
which she had not either feared or hoped to
see him; and it was to her a melancholy
thought that chance could no longer make
her meet him.

She went to Coulommiers, taking with her
copies she had had made of the large
pictures with which Madame de Valentinois
had adorned her fine house at Anet. All
the memorable events of the king's reign
were represented in these pictures. Among
others was one of the Siege of Metz, with
excellent likenesses of the principal officers,
among whom was Monsieur de Nemours; and
that was perhaps why Madame de Clèves
cared for the pictures.

Madame de Martigues, having been unable

to accompany the court, promised to spend a few days with her at Coulommiers. The queen's favor, which they both enjoyed, did not make them jealous or hostile; they were good friends, although they did not confide to each other everything. Madame de Clèves knew that Madame de Martigues loved the Vidame, but Madame de Martigues did not know that Madame de Clèves loved Monsieur de Nemours and was loved by him The fact that she was a niece of the Vidame endeared her to Madame de Martigues; and Madame de Clèves was drawn toward her as a woman who, like herself, was in love, and with her lover's most intimate friend.

Madame de Martigues kept her promise, and went to Coulommiers. She found Madame de Clèves leading a most retired life, — indeed, she had sought absolute solitude, spending her evenings in the gardens, unaccompanied by her servants. She used to go into the summer-house where Monsieur de Nemours had overheard her talking with her husband, and enter the closet which opened on the garden. Her women and the servants would stay in the summer-house or in the other closet, coming to her only when they were called. Madame de Martigues had never seen Coulommiers; she was delighted with all the loveliness she found there, and especially with the comfort of this summer-house, in which she and Madame de Clèves spent every evening. Their solitude after dark, in the most beautiful place in the world, made easy prolonged talks between these two young women, who were both in love; and although they did not confide in each other, they delighted in talking together. Madame de Martigues would have been very sorry to leave Coulommiers if she had not been going to meet the Vidame; she went to Chambort, where was the whole court.

The new king was crowned at Rheims by the Cardinal of Lorraine, and the rest of the summer was to be spent at the castle of Chambort, then newly built. The queen manifested great pleasure at seeing Madame de Martigues again; and after giving expression to her joy, she asked after Madame de Clèves and what she was doing in the country. Monsieur de Nemours and Monsieur de Clèves were then with the queen. Madame de Martigues, who had been delighted with Coulommiers, described its beauty, and spoke at great length of the summer-house in the wood and of the pleasant evenings she had passed there with Madame de Clèves. Monsieur de Nemours, who was sufficiently familiar with the place to know what Madame de Martigues was talking about, thought that it might be possible to see Madame de Clèves there without being seen by her. He questioned Madame de Martigues, in order to get further information; and Monsieur de Clèves, who had kept his eyes on him while Madame de Martigues was talking, fancied that he detected his design. The questions that Monsieur de Nemours asked only strengthened his suspicions, so that he felt sure the duke intended to go to see his wife. He was right; this plan so attracted Monsieur de Nemours that after spending the night in devising plans to carry it into execution, the next morning he asked leave of the king to go to Paris on some pretext he had invented.

Monsieur de Clèves had no doubt about his reasons for going away, but he determined to seek information on his wife's conduct, and no longer to remain in cruel uncertainty. He desired to leave at the same time with Monsieur de Nemours, and from some place of concealment to discover what success he might have; but he feared lest their simultaneous absence might attract attention, or that Monsieur de Nemours might get wind of it and adopt other measures; so he determined to rely on one of the gentlemen in his suite, in whose fidelity and intelligence he felt confidence. He told him in what trouble he was, and what Madame de Clèves' virtue had been hitherto, and ordered

him to follow in Monsieur de Nemours' footsteps, to watch him closely, and to see if he
did not go to Coulommiers and enter the
garden by night.

This gentleman, who was well suited for
the duty, discharged it with the utmost
exactness. He followed Monsieur de Nemours to a village half a league from
Coulommiers, where the prince stopped, and
the gentleman easily guessed that this was to
await the approach of night. He did not
think it well to wait there too, but passed
through the village and made his way into
the forest, to a spot which he thought Monsieur de Nemours would have to pass. He
was not mistaken; as soon as night had
fallen, he heard footsteps, and though it was
dark, he easily recognized Monsieur de
Nemours. He saw him walk about the garden
as if to find out if he could hear some one, and
to choose the most convenient spot for
entering it. The palings were very high, and
there were some beyond to bar the way, so

that it was not easy to get in; nevertheless, Monsieur de Nemours succeeded. As soon as he had made his way into the garden, he had no difficulty in making out where Madame de Clèves was, as he saw many lights in the closet. All the windows were open; and creeping along the palings, he approached it with an emotion that can easily be imagined. He hid behind one of the long windows by which one entered the closet, to see what Madame de Clèves was doing. He saw that she was alone; she was so beautiful that he could scarcely control his rapture at the spectacle. It was warm, and her head and shoulders had no other covering than her loosely fastened hair. She was on a couch behind a table, on which were many baskets of ribbons; she was picking some out, and Monsieur de Nemours observed that they were of the same colors that he had worn in the tournament. He saw that she was fastening bows on a very peculiar stick that he had carried for some time and had given

to his sister, from whom Madame de Clèves
had taken it, without seeming to recognize
it as belonging to Monsieur de Nemours.
When she had finished her work with a grace
and gentleness that reflected on her face the
feelings that filled her heart, she took a light
and drew near to a large table opposite the
picture of the Siege of Metz, in which was
the portrait of Monsieur de Nemours; then
she sat down and gazed at this portrait with
a rapt attention such as love alone could
give.

It would be impossible to describe everything that Monsieur de Nemours felt at this
moment. To see, in the deep night, in the
most beautiful spot in the world, the woman
he adored; to see her without her seeing
him, busied with things that bore reference
to him and to the hidden love she felt for
him, — all that is something no other lover
ever enjoyed or imagined.

Monsieur de Nemours was so entranced
that he stood motionless, contemplating

Madame de Clèves, without remembering that every moment was precious. When he had come to his senses again, he thought he ought to wait till she came into the garden before speaking to her; this he reflected would be safer, because then she would be farther from her maids. When, however, he saw that she remained in the closet, he decided to go in there. When he tried to do it, he was overwhelmed with agitation and with the fear of displeasing her. He could not bear the thought of seeing the face, just before so gentle, suddenly darken with anger and surprise.

He thought it madness, not his undertaking to see Madame de Clèves without being seen, but to think of showing himself; he saw everything that he had not before thought of. It seemed to him foolhardy to surprise at midnight a woman to whom he had never spoken of his love. He thought he had no right to assume that she would consent to listen to him, and he knew she would have good grounds for indignation at the danger to which he exposed her from the possible consequences of his acts. All his courage abandoned him, and more than once he was on the point of deciding that he would go back without seeing her. But he was so anxious to speak to her, and so encouraged by what he had seen, that he pushed on a few steps, though in such agitation that his scarf caught on the window and made a noise. Madame de Clèves turned her head; and whether it was that her mind was full of this prince, or that his face was actually in the light, she thought that she recognized him; and without hesitation or turning toward him, she rejoined her maids. She was so agitated that she had to trump up an excuse of not feeling well; and she said it also to attract their attention and thus give Monsieur de Nemours time to beat a retreat. After a little reflection she decided that she had been mistaken, and that the vision of Monsieur de Nemours was a mere illusion. She knew that he had been at Chambort, and she judged it extremely unlikely that he could have undertaken so perilous an enterprise; several times she was on the point of going back into the closet to see if there was any one in the garden. Perhaps she hoped as much as she feared to find Monsieur de Nemours there; but at last reason and prudence prevailed over every other feeling, and she decided that she should do better to stay where she was than to seek any further information. She was long in making up her mind to leave a place near which he might be, and it was almost morning when she returned to the castle.

Monsieur de Nemours stayed in the garden as long as he saw a light. He had not given up all hope of seeing Madame de Clèves again, although he was sure that she had recognized him and had only left in order to avoid him; but when he saw the servants locking the doors, he knew that he had no further chance. He retraced his steps, passing by the place where the friend of Monsieur de Clèves was in waiting. This gentleman followed him to the village, whence he had started in the evening. Monsieur de Nemours determined to spend the whole day there, in order to return to Coulommiers that night, to see if Madame de Clèves would be cruel enough to flee from him, or not to let him look at her. Although he was highly delighted to find that her mind was occupied with him, he was deeply pained to see her so instinctively taking flight.

Never was there a tenderer or intenser love than that which animated this prince He strolled beneath the willows beside a little brook which ran behind the house in which he was concealed. He kept himself out of sight as much as possible, that no one might know of his presence. He gave himself up to the transports of love, and his heart was so full that he could not keep from shedding a few tears; but these were not of grief, they were tempered with all the sweetness that only love can give.

He recalled all Madame de Clèves' actions since he had fallen in love with her, — the honorable and modest severity with which she had treated him, although she loved him. " For she does indeed love me," he exclaimed; "she loves me, — I cannot doubt it. The most fervent protestations, the greatest favors, are no surer tokens than those I have received; and yet she treats me with the same austerity as if she hated me. I thought time would bring a change, but I can expect nothing more from it; I see her always on her guard against me and against herself. If she did not love me, I should try to please her; but I do please her, she loves me, and hides her love. What then am I to hope, — what change in my fate can I expect. What! the most charming woman in the world loves me, and I cannot enjoy the supreme happiness that comes from the first certainty of being loved, except in the agony of being ill treated! Show. fair princess," he called aloud, " that you love me; show

me what you really feel! If you will only
once let me hear from you what your feelings
are, I am willing that you should resume for-
ever the severity with which you overwhelm
me. At least look at me with those eyes that I
saw gazing at my portrait. Could you look
at it with such gentleness, and then flee from
me so cruelly? What do you fear? Why
do you so dread my love? You love me,
and you hide your love to no purpose; you
have yourself given me tokens of it unawares.
I know my good fortune: let me enjoy it,
and cease making me unhappy. Is it
possible that Madame de Clèves loves me,
and I am still unhappy? How beautiful she
was last night! How could I resist my long-
ing to fling myself at her feet? Had I done
so, I might have prevented her flight; my
respectful bearing would have reassured her.
But perhaps she did not recognize me, — I
distress myself more than I should; and the
sight of a man at such an extraordinary hour
frightened her."

These thoughts haunted Monsieur de
Nemours all day.   He awaited the night
with impatience, and when it had come he
took once more the road to Coulommiers.   The
friend of Monsieur de Clèves, having assumed a disguise to avoid being recognized,
followed him as he had done the previous
evening, and saw him enter the same garden.
Then Monsieur de Nemours preceived that
Madame de Clèves was unwilling to run the
risk of his trying to see her; every entrance
was closed.   He wandered in every direction
to find some light, but his search was vain.

Madame de Clèves, suspecting that Monsieur de Nemours might come back, stayed
in her own room; she feared lest strength to
flee should be denied her, and she did not
wish to risk the possibility of speaking to
him in a manner that might contradict her
previous conduct.   Although Monsieur de
Nemours had no hope of seeing her, he
could not make up his mind to leave at once
a place where she had been so often.   He

spent the whole night in the garden, finding some slight consolation in at least gazing on the same objects which she saw every day. The sun had risen before he thought of leaving; but at last the fear of being observed compelled him to go

It was impossible for him to return without seeing Madame de Clèves; hence he went to see Madame de Mercœur, who was then living in her house not far from Coulommiers. She was extremely surprised at her brother's arrival. He invented some specious excuse for his journey, which completely deceived her, and at last managed so cleverly that she herself proposed their calling on Madame de Clèves. This plan they carried out that very day, and Monsieur de Nemours told his sister that he would leave her at Coulommiers to return with all speed to the king. He devised this plan of parting from her at Coulommiers in the hope that she would be the first to leave; in this way he imagined he could not fail to have an opportunity of speaking to Madame de Clèves.

When they reached Coulommiers, they found Madame de Clèves walking in a broad path along the edge of the flower-garden. The sight of Monsieur de Nemours embarrassed her not a little, and made her sure that it was he whom she had seen the previous night. This conviction filled her with anger that he should have been so bold and imprudent. He noticed with pain her evident coldness. The talk ran on insignificant subjects, and yet he succeeded in displaying so much wit and amiability, and so much admiration for Madame de Clèves, that he finally dispelled some of her coolness, in spite of her determination not to be appeased.

When he had got over his first timidity, he expressed great curiosity to see the summer-house in the wood; he described it as the most delightful spot in the world, and with so many details that Madame de Mercœur said he must have often seen it, to be so familiar with all its beauty.

"Still, I do not believe," answered Madame de Clèves, "that Monsieur de Nemours has ever been in it; it has been finished only a very short time."

"It is not long, either, since I was there," he retorted, looking at her; "and I do not know whether I ought not to be very glad that you have forgotten having seen me there."

Madame de Mercœur, who was busy looking at the garden, paid no attention to what her brother was saying. Madame de Clèves, blushing, and casting down her eyes so as not to see Monsieur de Nemours, said:

"I do not remember ever having seen you there, and if you ever have been there, it was without my knowledge."

"It is true, Madame," he said, "that I have been there without your permission, and I have spent there the most blissful and the most wretched moments of my life."

Madame de Clèves knew only too well what he meant; but she made no answer. She was thinking how she should keep Madame de Mercœur from going into the closet which contained the portrait of Monsieur de Nemours: this she did not want her to see. She succeeded so well that the time passed imperceptibly, and Madame de Mercœur spoke of leaving; but when Madame de Clèves noticed that Madame de Mercœur and her brother were not going away together, she saw the impending danger, and was as much embarrassed as she had been in Paris, and she decided on the same course. Her fear lest this visit should only confirm her husband's suspicions helped her to form this decision, and in order to prevent Monsieur de Nemours from being alone with her, she told Madame de Mercœur that she would accompany her to the edge of the forest, and ordered her carriage to follow her. This prince's grief at finding Madame de Clèves as austere as ever was so keen that he

turned pale. Madame de Mercœur asked
him if he was ill; but he looked at Madame
de Clèves without being seen by any one,
and let her see that he was suffering from
nothing but despair. Nevertheless, he was
compelled to let them go without daring to
follow them; and after what he had said,
he could not go back with his sister. He
returned to Paris, and left it the next day.

Monsieur de Clèves' friend had watched
him all the while. He also returned to Paris;
and when he saw that Monsieur de Nemours
had left for Chambort, he took the post
in order to get there before him, and to
make his report about his expedition. His
master was awaiting his return to determine
his life's unhappiness.

As soon as Monsieur de Clèves saw him,
he read in his expression and his silence
that he had brought only bad news. He
remained for some time overwhelmed with
grief, his head bowed, unable to speak; then
he motioned to him to withdraw. "Go,"

he said; "I see what you have to tell me, but I am not strong enough to hear it."

"I have nothing to report," answered the gentleman, "from which it is possible to form an accurate judgment. It is true that Monsieur de Nemours entered the garden in the woods two nights running, and called at Coulommiers the next day with Madame de Mercœur."

"That is enough," replied Monsieur de Clèves, "that is enough;" and then, again motioning to him to leave, he added, "I have no need of further information."

The gentleman was forced to leave his master plunged in despair. Never, perhaps, has there been more poignant grief, and few men who possessed so much spirit and so affectionate a heart as Monsieur de Clèves have suffered the agony of discovering at the same time a wife's infidelity and the mortification of being deceived by a woman.

Monsieur de Clèves was overwhelmed by this grievous blow. That same night he was seized with a fever of such severity that at once his life was in peril. Word was sent to Madame de Clèves, and she went to him with all speed. He was worse when she reached him, and she noticed something cold and icy in his manner toward her that greatly surprised and pained her. He even seemed to be annoyed at the attention she paid him; but at last she thought this was perhaps a result of his illness.

As soon as Madame de Clèves had arrived at Blois, where the court was at that time, Monsieur de Nemours was filled with joy at knowing that she was in the same place as himself. He tried to see her, and called at the house every day, under pretext of inquiring after Monsieur de Clèves; but it was all in vain. She never left her husband's room, and was very anxious about him. Monsieur de Nemours regretted that she suffered so much; he readily saw how this grief would be likely to rekindle her love for Monsieur de Clèves, and how this affection would prove a dangerous foe to the love she bore in her heart. This feeling depressed him for some time; but the extreme seriousness of Monsieur de Clèves' illness soon gave him new hopes He saw that Madame de Clèves would soon be free to follow her own wishes, and that in the future he might find lasting happiness. This thought filled him with almost painful rapture, and he banished it from his mind, lest he should be too miserable if his hopes were disappointed.

Meanwhile Monsieur de Clèves was almost given up. One of the last days of his illness, after he had passed a very bad night, he said, toward morning, that he would like to rest. Madame de Clèves alone stayed in his room. It seemed to her that instead of resting, he was very uneasy; she went up to him and knelt down by his bed, with her face covered with tears. Monsieur de Clèves had made up his mind to say nothing about his grievance against her; but her attentions and her sorrow, which seemed genuine, and which he sometimes regarded as tokens of deceit and treachery, produced such conflicting and painful feelings that he could not repress them.

"You, Madame," he said, "are shedding a great many tears for a death of which you are the cause, and which cannot give you the sorrow which you display. I am no longer able to reproach you," he went on, in a voice weakened by illness and grief, "but I am dying of the cruel suffering you have inflicted on me. Was it necessary that so extraordinary an action as that of speaking to me as you did at Coulommiers should have so little result? Why confide to me your love for Monsieur de Nemours, if your virtue was not strong enough to resist it? I loved you so that I was glad to be deceived, — I confess it to my shame; I have since longed for the false tranquillity of which you robbed me. Why did you not leave me in the calm blindness in which so many husbands are happy? I should perhaps have never known

that you loved Monsieur de Nemours.   I am
dying," he went on; "but bear it in mind
that you make me welcome death, and that
since you have robbed me of the love and
esteem I felt for you, I dread living.   What
would life be to me, if I had to spend it with
a woman I have loved so much and who has
so cruelly deceived me, or if I had to live
apart from her, after a scene of violence
utterly repugnant to my disposition and to
the love I bear you?   My love for you, Madame, has been far deeper than you know; I
have concealed the greater part of it, from
fear of tormenting you or of lessening your
esteem by a manner unbecoming to a husband; I really deserved your affection.   I say
it once more: I die without regret, since I
could not win this, and now can no longer
wish for it.   Farewell, Madame.   Some day
you will mourn a man who had for you a true
and lawful love.   You will know the misery
that overtakes women who fall into these en-
tanglements, and you will learn the difference

between being loved as I loved you, and being loved by men who, while protesting their love, seek only the honor of misleading you. But my death will leave you free, and you will be able to make Monsieur de Nemours happy without doing anything criminal. What do I care what may happen when I shall be no more? Must I be weak enough to look upon it?"

Madame de Clèves was so far from imagining that her husband could suspect her that she listened to him without understanding what he was saying, and supposing that he was blaming her interest in Monsieur de Nemours. At last, suddenly grasping his meaning, she exclaimed,—

"I a criminal! The very thought of it never entered my head. The severest virtue could command no different course of conduct than mine, and I have not done one thing of which I should not be glad to have you an eye-witness."

"Should you have been glad," asked

Monsieur de Clèves, looking at her somewhat disdainfully, "to have had me for an
eye-witness of the nights you spent with
Monsieur de Nemours? Ah! Madame, am
I speaking of you when I speak of a woman
who has spent nights with a man?"

"No," she answered, "no; it is not of
me that you are speaking, — I have never
passed nights or moments with Monsieur
de Nemours; he has never seen me in
private; I have never had anything to do
with him or listened to him, and I will
swear — "

"Say no more," interrupted Monsieur de
Clèves; "false oaths or a confession would
give me equal pain."

Madame de Clèves could not answer; her
tears and her grief choked her. At last,
making a great effort, she said: "Look at
me, at least; listen to me. If it concerned
me alone, I should endure these reproaches;
but it is your life that is at stake. Listen to
me for your own sake; it is impossible that,

with all the truth on my side, I should not convince you of my innocence."

"Would to God that you could convince me!" he exclaimed. "But what can you say to me? Was not Monsieur de Nemours at Coulommiers with his sister, and had he not passed the two previous nights with you in the garden in the forest?"

"If that is my crime," she replied, "I can clear myself easily. I don't ask you to believe me, but believe your servants: ask them if I was in the garden the evening Monsieur de Nemours came to Coulommiers, and if I did n't leave it the evening before, two hours earlier than usual."

She then told him how she had imagined she saw some one in the garden, and confessed that she had thought it was Monsieur de Nemours. She spoke with such earnestness, and the truth, even when improbable, carries such weight, that Monsieur de Clèves was almost convinced of her innocence.

"I do not know," he said, "whether I dare

believe you; I am so near death that I do not want to see anything that might make me long to live. Your explanation comes too late; but it will always be a consolation to think that you are worthy of the esteem I have had for you. I beg of you to let me have the additional consolation of knowing that my memory will be dear to you, and that if it had depended on you, you would have had for me the feeling you have had for another."

He wanted to go on; but a sudden faintness made it impossible, and Madame de Clèves summoned the physicians. They found him almost lifeless. Nevertheless, he lingered a few days longer, and at last died, having displayed admirable firmness.

Madame de Clèves was almost crazed by the intensity of her grief. The queen at once came to see her, and carried her to a convent, without her knowing whither she was going. Her sisters-in-law brought her to Paris before she was yet able to realize her afflictions. When she began to be strong enough to think about it, and saw what a husband she had lost, and reflected that she was the cause of his death by means of her love for another man, the horror she felt at herself and at Monsieur de Nemours cannot be described.

At first this prince did not venture to pay her any other attentions than such as etiquette required. He knew Madame de Clèves well enough to be sure that anything more marked would displease her; but what he learned later assured him that he would have to maintain this reserve for a long time. One of his equerries told him that Monsieur de Clèves' gentleman, a friend of his, had told him, in his deep regret for the loss of his master, that Monsieur de Nemours' trip to Coulommiers was the cause of his death. Monsieur de Nemours was extremely surprised to hear this; but on thinking it over, he made out a part of the truth, and conjectured what would be the feelings of Madame de Clèves, and how she would detest him if she thought her husband's illness had been due to jealousy. He thought that the best thing would be not to have his name brought to her notice, and he regulated his conduct accordingly, painful as he found it.

The prince went to Paris, and could not refrain from calling on Madame de Clèves to ask how she was. He was informed that she saw no one, and had even given orders that she was not to be told who had inquired after her. Possibly these rigid orders were given solely on account of the prince, and to avoid hearing his name mentioned. But Monsieur de Nemours was too desperately in love to be able to live with absolutely no chance of seeing Madame de Clèves. He resolved to try every means, no matter how difficult, to escape from such an unendurable condition of affairs.

The princess's grief passed all bounds of reason. Her dying husband, — dying for her sake, and filled with such tender love for her, — was never absent from her mind; she continually recalled everything she owed him, and blamed herself for not having loved him, — as if that were a thing that depended on her will. Her sole consolation was the thought that she mourned him as he deserved, and that for the rest of her life she would only do what he would have approved if he had lived.

She had often wondered how he knew that Monsieur de Nemours had come to Coulommiers; she did not suspect that the prince had spoken of it, and it even seemed to her that it was immaterial whether he had said anything about it, so thoroughly rid of her passion did she feel. Nevertheless, she was deeply distressed to think that he was the cause of her husband's death, and she remembered with sorrow the fear that had tormented Monsieur de Clèves on his deathbed lest she should marry him; but all these various sources of grief were lost in that over her husband's death, and the others sank into insignificance.

After many months had passed, she recovered from her violent grief, becoming sad and languid. Madame de Martigues made a visit to Paris, and saw her repeatedly during her stay there. She talked with her about the court and of all that had happened; and although Madame de Clèves seemed to take no interest, Madame de Martigues went on talking in order to divert her. She told her all about the Vidame, Monsieur de Guise, and all the other men of note.

"As for Monsieur de Nemours," she said, "I do not know whether his occupations have taken the place of gallantry, but he is less cheerful than he used to be; he shuns the society of women; he continually runs up to Paris, and I believe is here now."

Monsieur de Nemours' name surprised Madame de Clèves and made her blush;

she changed the subject, and Madame de Martigues did not notice her confusion.

The next day, the princess, being anxious to find some occupation suitable for her condition, went to see a man living close by who worked in silk in a peculiar way, with the intention of undertaking something of the sort herself. After looking at what he had to show, her eyes fell on the door of a room in which she thought there were some more, and asked to have it opened. The man replied that he did not have the key, and that it was occupied by a man who came there sometimes to draw the fine houses and gardens to be seen from the windows. " He is the handsomest man in the world," he went on, " and does not seem obliged to support himself by his work. Whenever he comes here, I see him always looking at the houses and gardens, but I have never seen him at work."

Madame de Clèves listened with great attention; what Madame de Martigues had said

about Monsieur de Nemours coming sometimes to Paris, as well as her vision of this
handsome man who had taken quarters near
her house, made her think of that prince,
and suggested that he was trying to see her.
This thought produced in her an agitation
which she could not understand. She went
to the windows to see on what they looked,
and saw that it was on her garden and her
own apartment; and when she was in her
room she saw the same window to which she
had been told that the stranger used to come.
The conjecture that it was Monsieur de Nemours entirely altered the current of her
thoughts; she no longer felt the sad tranquillity which she had begun to enjoy, — she
was uneasy and agitated. At last, unable to
endure her loneliness, she went out to take
the air in a garden in the faubourgs, where
she expected to find solitude. At first she
supposed no one was there; the place seemed
deserted, and she strolled about for some
little time.

After passing through a little thicket, she saw at the end of the path, in the most retired part of the garden, a sort of summer-house open on all sides, and she turned in that direction. When she had got near it, she saw a man lying on the benches who seemed sunk in deep thought, and she recognized Monsieur de Nemours. At the sight of him she stopped short; but her servants, who were following her, made some noise that aroused him. Without looking at them, he arose, to avoid their company, and turned into another path, bowing deeply, so that he was unable to see whom he was saluting.

Had Monsieur de Nemours known from whom he was running away, he would have eagerly retraced his steps; but as it was, he followed the path and went out by a side-gate, at which his carriage was waiting. This incident made a deep impression on Madame de Clèves' heart; all her love was suddenly rekindled with its former fervor. She went

on and sat down in the place which Monsieur
de Nemours had just left, and there she remained, completely overwhelmed. Her mind
was full of this prince, more fascinating than
any man in the world; loving her long with
respect and constancy; giving up everything
for her; respecting even her grief; trying
to see her, without himself being seen;
abandoning the court, where he was a favorite,
to look upon the walls behind which she was
immured, to come and muse in places where
he could not hope to meet her, — in short, a
man worthy to be loved for his love alone,
and for whom she felt a passion so violent
that she would have loved him even if he
had not loved her, and one moreover of
a lofty nature perfectly in harmony with her
own. Duty and virtue could not restrain her
emotions; every obstacle vanished; and of
all her past she remembered nothing but
her love for Monsieur de Nemours and his
for her.

All these thoughts were new to the

princess; she had been so lost in grief for her husband's death that she had given them no attention. With the sight of Monsieur de Nemours they all recurred to her. But when they came fastest, and she remembered that this same man whom now she thought of as able to marry her was the one she had loved during her husband's lifetime and was the cause of his death; that on his deathbed he had manifested his fear lest she should marry him, — her rigid virtue was so pained by the thought that it seemed to her quite as grievous a crime to marry Monsieur de Nemours as it had been to love him while her husband was living. She gave herself up to these reflections, which were so hostile to her happiness, and confirmed them by many arguments concerning her peace of mind and the evils she foresaw in case she married him. At last, after spending two hours there, she returned home, convinced that she ought to avoid the sight of him as a real obstacle to her duty.

But this conviction, the product of reason and virtue, did not control her heart, which remained attached to Monsieur de Nemours with a violence that reduced her to a most restless and pitiable state. That night was one of the unhappiest she had ever known. In the morning her first thought was to go to see if there was any one at the window which commanded her house; she looked out and saw Monsieur de Nemours. This surprised her, and she drew back so quickly that he felt sure she must have recognized him. This he had long wished might happen, since he had devised this method of seeing her; and when it seemed hopeless, he used to go and meditate in the garden where she had seen him.

Worn out at last by grief and uncertainty, the duke made up his mind to find some way of determining his fate. "Why should I wait?" he asked. "I have long known she loved me; she is free, and duty no longer stands in her way. Why should she force me to see her without being seen by her and with no chance to speak to her? Can love have so absolutely destroyed my reason and my boldness that I am not what I was when in love before? I was bound to respect Madame de Clèves' grief; but I have respected it too long, and I am giving her time to forget the affection she feels for me."

Thereupon he began to devise some way of seeing her. He fancied that there was no good reason for concealing his love from the Vidame of Chartres, and he resolved to speak to him and to confide to him his plans about his niece. The Vidame was then in Paris, like all the rest of the court, who had come to town to make their preparations for accompanying the king, who was to escort the Queen of Spain. Accordingly, Monsieur de Nemours called on the Vidame and frankly told him everything he had kept hidden until then, except Madame de Clèves' feelings, which he did not wish to appear to know.

The Vidame heard him with great pleasure, and answered that, with no knowledge of his feelings, he had often, since Madame de Clèves had become a widow, thought that she was the only woman worthy of him. Monsieur de Nemours besought his aid in getting a chance to address her, in order to find out her intentions.

The Vidame proposed taking him to call on her; but Monsieur de Nemours feared that she would not like this, because she did not yet see any one. They decided that the Vidame should invite her to come and see him on some pretext or other, and that Monsieur de Nemours should enter by a hidden staircase, in order not to be seen. This was carried out according to their plans. Madame de Clèves came; the Vidame went to receive her, and led her into a small room at the end of his apartment. Shortly after, Monsieur de Nemours came in, as if by chance. Madame de Clèves was much surprised to see him; she blushed, and tried to hide her blushes. The Vidame began to talk about unimportant subjects, and then went away, under the pretext of having some orders to give. He asked Madame de Clèves to do the honors in his place, and said he should return in a moment.

It would be impossible to express the feelings of Monsieur de Nemours and Madame de Clèves when they for the first time found themselves alone and free to talk. They remained for a long time without a word; then at last Monsieur de Nemours broke the silence. "Will you, Madame, forgive the Vidame," he said, "for having given me an opportunity to see you and to speak with you, which you have always cruelly denied me?"

"I ought not to forgive him," she replied, "for having forgotten my position and to what he exposes my reputation." As she uttered these words she started to leave; but Monsieur de Nemours delayed her, saying:

"Do not be alarmed, Madame; no one

knows that I am here, and there is no danger. Listen to me, Madame, — if not through kindness, at least through love of yourself, and in order to protect yourself against the extravagances to which I shall certainly be led by an uncontrollable passion."

For the first time Madame de Clèves yielded to her tenderness for Monsieur de Nemours, and looking at him with eyes full of gentleness and charm, she said: "But what do you hope from the kindness that you ask of me? You would certainly regret obtaining it, and I should regret granting it. You deserve a happier fate than you have yet had, and can have in the future, unless you seek it elsewhere."

"I, Madame, find such happiness elsewhere! Is there any other happiness than winning your love? Although I have never spoken with you, I cannot think that you are ignorant of my affection, or that you do not know that it is truer and warmer than ever. How much it has been tried by events unknown to you, and how much by your severity!"

"Since you wish me to speak, and I decide it best," answered Madame de Clèves, sitting down, "I will do so, with a frankness that you will not always find in women. I shall not tell you that I have not noticed your attachment to me, — perhaps you could not believe me if I were to say so; I confess, then, not only that I have noticed it, but also just as you wished it to appear."

"And, Madame, if you have seen it," he interrupted, "is it possible that you have not been touched by it; and may I venture to ask if it has made no impression on your heart?"

"You should have judged of that from my conduct," she replied; "but I should be glad to know what you have thought of it."

"I should have to be in a happier condition to dare to tell you," he answered, "and my fate has too little relation with what

I should say. All that I can tell you, Madame, is that you would not have confessed to Monsieur de Clèves what you concealed from me, and that you would have concealed from him what you would have let me see."

"How were you able to find out," she asked, blushing, "that I confessed anything to Monsieur de Clèves?"

"I heard it from your own lips, Madame," he replied; "but as an excuse for my boldness in listening to you, consider whether I misused what I had heard, whether my hopes were strengthened by it, whether I became bold enough to speak to you."

He began to tell her how he had heard her conversation with Monsieur de Clèves; but she interrupted him in the middle.

"Say no more," she said; "I now see how you came to know too much: that you did, was very plain to me at the dauphiness's, when she had heard the story from those to whom you had told it."

Monsieur de Nemours then explained to her how that had happened.

"Do not apologize," she resumed; "I forgave you a long time ago, before you told me how it occurred. But since you have yourself heard from me what I had meant to keep a secret from you all my life, I confess that you have inspired me with emotions unknown before I saw you, and so unfamiliar to me that they filled me with a surprise which greatly added to the agitation they produced. I confess this with the less shame because I may now do it innocently, and you have seen that my feelings did not guide my actions."

"Do you believe, Madame," exclaimed Monsieur de Nemours, falling on his knees, "that I am not ready to die at your feet with joy and rapture?"

"I only tell you," she answered, smiling, "what you already know only too well."

"Ah! Madame," he said, "what a difference between finding something out by accident, and hearing it from you, and seeing that you wish me to know it."

"It is true," said she, "that I wish you to know it, and that I take pleasure in telling you. I am not certain that I do not tell it more from love of myself than from love of you; for certainly this avowal will have no consequences, and I shall follow the rigid rules that my condition imposes."

"You will not think of such a thing, Madame," replied Monsieur de Nemours; "you are bound by no further duty; you are free; and if I dared, I should even tell you that it depends on you so to act that your duty shall some day oblige you to preserve the feelings that you have for me."

"My duty," she replied, "forbids my ever thinking of any one, and of you last of all, for reasons unknown to you."

"Perhaps they are not, Madame," he pleaded; "but those are no true reasons. I have reason to believe that Monsieur de Clèves thought me happier than I was, and imagined that you approved of mad freaks of mine which my passion suggested without your knowledge."

"Let us not speak of that affair," she said. "I cannot bear the thought of it; it fills me with shame, and its consequences were too painful. It is only too likely that you are the cause of Monsieur de Clèves' death; the suspicions you aroused, your inconsiderate conduct, cost him his life as truly as if you had taken it with your own hands. Think of what I should do if you had come to such extremities and the same unhappy result had followed. I know very well this is not the same thing in the eyes of the world; but in mine there is no difference, for I know it was from you he got his death, and on account of me."

"Oh! Madame," interposed Monsieur de Nemours, "what phantom of duty do you oppose to my happiness? What! Madame, a vain and baseless fancy can prevent your making happy a man you do not hate, when he has conceived the hope of passing his life with you, his fate leading him to love you as the best woman in the world, finding in you every charming trait, incurring not your hatred, and seeing in you everything that best becomes a woman, — for, Madame, there is no other woman who combines what you do. Men who marry their mistresses who love them, tremble from fear lest they should renew their misconduct with others; but nothing of the sort is to be feared in you: you are only to be admired. Can I have foreseen such felicity only to find you raising obstacles? Ah! Madame, you forget that you chose me from other men, — or rather, you did not; you made a mistake, and I have flattered myself."

" You did not flatter yourself," she replied; " the reasons for my acting as I do would not, perhaps, seem to me so strong, had I not chosen you as you suspect, — and that is what makes me foresee unhappiness if I should take an interest in you."

"I have no answer," he said, "when you show me that you fear unhappiness; but I confess that, after all you have been good enough to say to me, I did not expect to be opposed by such a cruel argument."

"It is so far from uncomplimentary to you," she answered, "that I shall even find it hard to tell it to you."

"Alas! Madame, what can you fear will flatter me too much after what you have just said to me?"

"I wish still to speak to you as frankly as I began," she explained, "and I want to dispense with all the reserve and formalities that I should respect in a first conversation; but I beg of you to listen to me without interruption.

"I think it but a slight reward for your affection that I should hide from you none of my feelings, but should let you see them exactly as they are. This probably will be the only time in my life that I shall take the liberty of letting you see them; neverthe-

less, I cannot confess to you without deep
shame that the certainty of not being loved
by you as I am, seems to me a horrible
misfortune; that if there were not already
insurmountable claims of duty, I doubt if I
could make up my mind to risk this unhappiness. I know that you are free, as I am,
and that we are so situated that the world
would probably blame neither of us if we
should marry; but do men keep their love in
these permanent unions? Ought I to expect a miracle in my case, and can I run the
risk of seeing this passion, which would be
my only happiness, fade away? Monsieur
de Clèves was perhaps the only man in the
world capable of keeping his love after marriage. My fate forbade my enjoying this
blessing. Perhaps, too, his love only sur-
vived because he found none in me. But
I should not have the same way of preserv-
ing yours; I believe that the obstacles you
have met have made you constant; those
were enough to make you yearn to conquer

them, and my involuntary actions, — things you learned by chance, — gave you enough hope to keep you interested."

"Oh! Madame," replied Monsieur de Nemours, "I can no longer maintain the silence you impose on me; you do me too much injustice, and you let me see how far you are from being prejudiced in my favor."

"I confess," she said, "that I may be moved by my emotions, but they cannot blind me; nothing can prevent my seeing that you are born with every disposition for gallantry, and with all the qualities proper to secure speedy success. You have already been in love several times, — you would be again very often. I should not make you happy; I should see you interested in another as you have been in me: this would inflict on me a mortal blow, and I should never feel sure that I should not be jealous. I have said too much to try to hide from you that you have already made me feel this passion, and that I suffered cruel tortures

that evening when the queen gave me that
letter from Madame de Themines which was
said to be directed to you, and that the
impression left on me is that jealousy is
the greatest unhappiness in the world.

"Vanity or taste makes all women try to
secure you; there are few whom you do not
please,— my own experience teaches me that
there are few whom you might not please.
I should always imagine that you were loved
and in love, and I should not be often wrong.
Yet in this condition I could only suffer, —
I should not dare to complain. One may
make reproaches to a lover, but can a
woman reproach her husband for ceasing
to love her? If I could become hardened
to that misfortune, could I become hardened to imagining that I saw Monsieur de
Clèves charging you with his death, reproaching me for loving you, and showing the
difference between his affection and yours?
It is impossible to resist such arguments;
I must remain in my present position and

in my immovable determination never to leave it."

"But do you think you can, Madame?" exclaimed Monsieur de Nemours. "Do you think that your resolutions can hold out against a man who worships you and is fortunate enough to please you? It is harder than you think, Madame, to resist what pleases us and one who loves us. You have done it by an austere virtue which is almost without a precedent; but this virtue no longer conflicts with your emotions, and these I hope you will follow, in spite of yourself."

"I know that there is nothing harder than what I undertake; I mistrust my own strength, supported by all my arguments. What I think due to the memory of Monsieur de Clèves would be ineffectual, if it were not reinforced by my anxiety for my own peace of mind; and these arguments need to be strengthened by those of duty. But though I mistrust myself, I think I shall never overcome my scruples, and I do not hope to overcome my interest in you. It will make me unhappy, and I shall deny myself the pleasure of seeing you, whatever pain this may cost me. I am in a position which makes that a crime which at any other time would be permissible, and mere etiquette forbids that we should meet."

Monsieur de Nemours flung himself at her feet and gave expression to all the emotion that filled him. He manifested, by his words and tears, the liveliest and tenderest passion that heart ever felt. Madame de Clèves was not unmoved; and looking at Monsieur de Nemours with eyes heavy with tears, she exclaimed, —

"Why must I charge you with the death of Monsieur de Clèves? Why did I not learn to know you when I was free; or why did I not know you before I was married? Why does fate divide us by such an insuperable obstacle?"

"There is no obstacle," pleaded Monsieur de Nemours; "you alone thwart my happiness, you alone impose a law which virtue and reason could not impose."

"It is true," she replied, "that I make a great sacrifice to a duty which exists only in my imagination. Wait to see what time will do. Monsieur de Clèves has but just died, and that fatal event is too recent for me to judge clearly. Meanwhile you have the pleasure of having won the love of a woman who would never have loved had she not seen you; be sure that my feelings for you will never change and will always survive, whatever I do.

"Good by," she said. "This conversation fills me with shame. Repeat it to the Vidame; I give my consent, — nay, I beg of you to do so."

With these words she left the room, Monsieur de Nemours being unable to prevent her. She found the Vidame in the next room. He saw her so agitated that he did not dare to speak to her, and he handed her to her carriage without a word. He went back to Monsieur de Nemours, who was in such a whirl of joy, sadness, surprise, and admiration, — in short, so possessed by all the emotions that spring from a passion full of hope and dread, — that he seemed beside himself. It was long before the Vidame got any clear notion of what they had said; finally, however, he succeeded; and Monsieur de Chartres, without being the least in love, had no less admiration for the virtue, intelligence, and worth of Madame de Clèves than had Monsieur de Nemours himself. They tried to determine the prince's probable chances; and whatever the fears that love might arouse, the prince agreed with the Vidame that it was impossible that Madame de Clèves should persist in her resolutions. Nevertheless, they agreed to follow her orders, from fear lest, if the duke's love for her should become known, she should in some way bind herself, and would not change from fear of its being thought that she had loved him while her husband was living.

Monsieur de Nemours determined to join the king, as he could no longer stay away, and he made up his mind to start without even trying to see Madame de Clèves again. He begged the Vidame to speak to her. He told him a number of things to say to her, and suggested countless arguments with which to overcome her scruples. At last a good part of the night was gone before Monsieur de Nemours thought of leaving to seek repose.

Madame de Clèves was in no condition to find rest; it was for her such a new thing to lay aside the reserve which she had imposed upon herself, to permit a man to tell her that he loved her, to confess that she too was in love, that she did not recognize herself. She was amazed at what she had done, and repented it bitterly; she was also made happy by it, — she was completely upset by love and agitation. She went over once more the arguments in defence of her duty which stood in the way of her happiness; she lamented their strength, and regretted having stated them so strongly to Monsieur de Nemours. Although the thought of marrying him had occurred to her the moment she saw him again in the garden, it had not made so deep an impression on her as had her talk with him; and at moments she could scarcely believe that she would be unhappy if she should marry him. She would have liked to be able to say that she was wrong both in her scruples about the past and in her fears for the future. At other moments reason and duty convinced her of the opposite, and decided her not to marry again or ever to see Monsieur de Nemours; but this resolution was extremely repugnant to her when her heart was so much moved and had so recently seen the joys of love. At last, in order to allay her agitation, she thought it was not necessary for her to do herself the violence of forming a decision, — etiquette left her still much time for making up her mind; but she resolved to abide by her determination to have nothing to do with Monsieur de Nemours meanwhile.

The Vidame came to see her, and pleaded his friend's cause with all possible skill and earnestness; but he could not persuade her to modify her own conduct or that which she had imposed on Monsieur de Nemours. She told him that she did not mean to change her present condition, that she knew it would be hard for her to carry out this intention, but that she hoped she should be strong enough to do so. She showed him how firmly convinced she was that Monsieur de Nemours had caused her husband's death, and that she should do wrong in marrying him; so that the Vidame feared it would not be easy to convince her of the opposite. He did not confide to this prince what he thought, and when he reported his talk with her, he let him enjoy all the hope that reason can awaken in a man who is loved.

The next day they left to join the king. The Vidame, at the request of Monsieur de Nemours, wrote to Madame de Clèves, in order to speak of him; and in a second letter, which soon followed, Monsieur de Nemours added a few lines himself. But Madame de Clèves, who did not wish to infringe her rules, and who feared the perils of correspondence, told the Vidame that she should decline to receive his letters if he continued to write about Monsieur de Nemours; and this she said so earnestly that this prince himself begged his friend never to mention his name.

The court left to escort the Queen of Spain as far as Poitou. Madame de Clèves was left to herself during their absence, and the farther she was removed from Monsieur de Nemours and from anything that could remind her of him, the more she recalled the memory of Monsieur de Clèves, which she was bent on keeping ever present before her. Her reasons for not marrying Monsieur de Nemours seemed strong so far as her duty, and irrefutable so far as her tranquillity, was concerned. The fading of his love after marriage, and all the pangs of jealousy, which she regarded as certain, showed her the misery to which she would expose herself; but she saw too that she had assumed an impossible task in undertaking to resist the most fascinating of men, whom she loved and who loved her, in a matter which offended neither virtue nor propriety. She decided that only separation could give her strength; and this she felt that she needed, not merely to maintain her determination not to marry, but also to protect herself from the sight of Monsieur de Nemours. Hence she resolved to make a long journey during the time that etiquette forced her to spend in retirement. Some large estates that she owned in the Pyrenees seemed to her the best place she could choose. She started a few days before the court returned; and just before leaving, she wrote to the Vidame to beg that no one should inquire after her or write to her.

Monsieur de Nemours was as much afflicted by her absence as another man

would have been by the death of the woman
he loved. The thought of this long separation from Madame de Clèves was a constant
source of suffering, especially after he had
tasted the pleasure of meeting her and seeing that she loved him. He could do nothing but grieve, and his grief increased daily.
Madame de Clèves, as a result of all her
agitation, fell seriously ill after her arrival at
her country place, and news of this reached
the court. Monsieur de Nemours was in-
consolable, and fell into the most unbounded
despair. The Vidame had great difficulty in
keeping him from letting his love be seen, as
well as from following after her to find out
how she was. The Vidame's relationship and
intimacy served as a pretext for sending
constant letters. At last word came that
she had passed the turning point of her
dangerous illness, but was still so weak that
all were very anxious.

This long and near view of death enabled
Madame de Clèves to judge mundane matters
in a very different spirit from that of health.

Her imminent peril taught her indifference to everything, and the length of her illness enforced this upon her. Yet when she had recovered, she found that she had not wholly forgotten Monsieur de Nemours; but she summoned to her aid every argument she could devise against marrying him. The conflict was a stern one; but at last she conquered what was left of this passion, which was already diminished by her reflections during her illness. The thought of death had revived her memory of Monsieur de Clèves; and this, harmonizing with her sense of duty, made a strong impression on her heart. The affections and ties of the world appeared to her as they appear to persons of enlarged views. Her health, which was still delicate, helped her to preserve those feelings; but knowing how circumstances affect the wisest resolutions, she was unwilling to run the risk of seeing her own altered, or of returning to the place where lived the man she had loved. Under the pretext of needing change of air, she withdrew to a religious house, without making known her determination to leave the court.

When Monsieur de Nemours heard of this, he at once saw what a decisive step it was, and feared that he had no more ground for hope. Yet the destruction of his hopes did not prevent his doing his utmost to bring about her return; he made the queen write to her, and even persuaded the Vidame to visit her: but it was all to no purpose. The Vidame saw her; she did not tell him that she had resolved upon this, but he decided that she would never return. At last Monsieur de Nemours went himself, under the pretext of going to the baths. She was much moved and astonished when she heard that he had come. She sent him a message by one of her trusty companions that she begged him not to be surprised if she was unwilling to run the risk of seeing him again and of having the feelings she felt bound to maintain swept away by his presence; that she wanted him to know that having found her duty and her peace of mind unalterably opposed to her interest in him, everything else in the world seemed so indifferent that she had abandoned it entirely, had given all her thoughts to another life, and had no other feeling left but her desire to have him share the same sentiments.

Monsieur de Nemours thought he should die of grief in the presence of the woman who brought this message. He begged her twenty times to go back to Madame de Clèves, to entreat her to let him see her; but she told him that Madame de Clèves had forbidden her, not only to bring her any message from him, but even to repeat to her what he might say. At last he had to leave, as completely overwhelmed with grief as a man could be who had lost all hopes of ever seeing again a woman whom he loved with the most violent and the most natural passion possible. Yet he did not yield even then; he did everything he could to induce her to alter her decision. At last, when years had passed, time and separation allayed his grief and extinguished his passion. Madame de Clèves led such a life that it was evident she meant never to go into the world again; part of each year she spent in this religious house, and the other part at home, but in retirement, busied with severer tasks than those of the austerest convents. Her life, which was not long, furnished examples of the loftest virtue.

CPSIA information can be obtained at www.ICGtesting.com
Printed in the USA
239270LV00002B/78/P